SCOTT FORESMAN

SiDEWALKS

Practice Book

Level B

PEARSON

Scott Foresman

Editorial Offices: Glenview, Illinois • Parsippany, New Jersey
New York, New York
Sales Offices: Boston, Massachusetts • Duluth, Georgia
Glenview, Illinois • Coppell, Texas • Sacramento, California • Mesa, Arizona

ISBN: 0-328-21383-7

10 V034 15 14 13 12 11 10 09 08
CC1

Contents

Name_____

Circle the word for each picture.
Write the word on the line.

b**a**t

---

cat   cot

1. _____

fun   fan

2. _____

---

map   mop

3. _____

big   bag

4. _____

---

cup   cap

5. _____

hat   hot

6. _____

---

cub   cab

7. _____

mat   met

8. _____

---

tug   tag

9. _____

pan   pen

10. _____

© Pearson Education B

School + Home

Home Activity This page practices words with the short *a* sound heard in *bat*. Work through the page with your child. Write *an*, *at*, *ad*, and *ap* on slips of paper. Help your child add beginning letters to form short *a* words.

Name_____

Circle the word for each picture.
Write the word on the line.

du<u>ck</u>

---

1. stop   sock

_____

- - - - - - - - - -

_____

2. tack   tap

_____

- - - - - - - - - -

_____

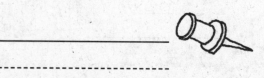

---

3. lock   lot

_____

- - - - - - - - - -

_____

4. bib   brick

_____

- - - - - - - - - -

_____

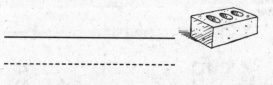

---

5. clock   cot

_____

- - - - - - - - - -

_____

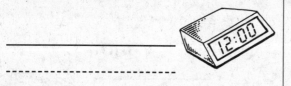

6. tug   truck

_____

- - - - - - - - - -

_____

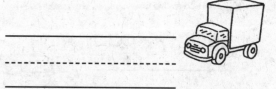

---

7. nest   neck

_____

- - - - - - - - - -

_____

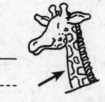

8. stick   sting

_____

- - - - - - - - - -

_____

© Pearson Education B

School + Home

Home Activity This lesson reviews words with the final *k* sound spelled *ck* (duck). Work through the items with your child. Then help your child write these words and tell what they mean: *track, snack, sick,* and *luck.*

Name_____

Read the story.

Look at the pictures.

Write 1, 2, 3, 4 to show the right order.

Dan was at bat. Then he got a hit. Next, Dan ran fast. Last, he will stand on the sack.

_____
- - - - - - - - - - - - - - - - - -
_____

_____
- - - - - - - - - - - - - - - - - -
_____

_____
- - - - - - - - - - - - - - - - - -
_____

_____
- - - - - - - - - - - - - - - - - -
_____

Write a sentence. Tell what Dan can do next.

_____
- -
_____

© Pearson Education B

Home Activity Your child numbers the events to show the order in which they happened. Tell your child a short story. Ask what happens *first, then, next,* and *last.*

Practice Book Unit 1

Comprehension Sequence **3**

Name_____

Pick a word from the box to finish each sentence.
Write the word on the line.
You will use one of the words twice.

> always   laugh   only   told

1. Val had two caps, but Pam _____ had one.

2. Val _____ Pam that one cap was too big.

3. Pam _____ Val that it would not fit.

4. They could _____ at the cap.

5. Pam and Val _____ have fun.

Home Activity This page helps your child learn the words *always*, *laugh*, *only*, and *told*. Ask your child to read the sentences to you. Then write the words *always*, *laugh*, *only*, and *told* on cards. Use the cards to help your child practice spelling and reading each word.

Name_____

Read each question.
Write a sentence to answer each question.

1. Where do you live?

_____

- -

_____

2. Who are your pals there?

_____

- -

_____

3. What can you see there?

_____

- -

_____

- -

_____

4. What do you like best about it?

_____

- -

_____

 Home Activity On this page, your child writes sentences. This gives your child practice in using capital letters and periods. Help your child write the sentences. Then read them together.

Name_____

Circle the word for each picture.
Write the word on the line.

ship

---

pin   pan

1. _____

peg   pig

2. _____

---

hit   hat

3. _____

wag   wig

4. _____

---

fan   fin

5. _____

sank   sink

6. _____

---

lid   led

7. _____

crab   crib

8. _____

---

last   list

9. _____

ring   rang

10. _____

© Pearson Education B

Home Activity This page practices words with the short *i* sound in *ship*. Review the page with your child. Then together find in your home something **big**, something **thin**, something **thick**, and something with the number **six**.

Name_____

Pick a word from the box to name each picture.
Write the word on the line.

bunk	drink	king
trunk	swing	wing

r<u>ng</u>   si<u>nk</u>

1.

_____

- - - - - - - - - - - - -

_____

2.

_____

- - - - - - - - - - - - -

_____

3.

_____

- - - - - - - - - - - - -

_____

4.

_____

- - - - - - - - - - - - -

_____

5.

_____

- - - - - - - - - - - - -

_____

6.

_____

- - - - - - - - - - - - -

_____

Find the word that has the same ending sound as the picture.

Mark the ⬭ to show your answer.

7. ⬭ thank
    ⬭ thing
    ⬭ then

8. ⬭ bang
    ⬭ best
    ⬭ bank

 Home Activity This page reviews words with the final sounds *ng* and *nk*, as in *ring* and *sink*. Work through the items with your child. Help your child write a sentence using one or more of the words. Have your child read aloud the sentence and draw a picture to illustrate it.

© Pearson Education B

Practice Book Unit 1

Name_____

Read the text.
Follow the directions.

"That is a blimp. A blimp can lift
up and away," Dad said.
"I wish I could go on a blimp," Liz said.
With a wink, Dad said, "I grant your wish."
Dad and Liz get in, and the blimp goes over hills.
Then they land. "That was the best trip!" said Liz.
"Thank you, Dad."

1. **Circle** the answer that gives the best title for the text.

   The Big Hills   Lift Up   A Trip in a Blimp

2. **Circle** the answer that tells the main idea.
   Liz and her dad ride in a blimp.
   A blimp can go over hills.

3. **Write** a sentence to tell a **detail** about the main idea.

   _____

   -

   _____

   -

   _____

Home Activity Your child identifies the main idea and a detail in a story. Ask your child to read the story to you and tell you the main idea, or what the story is all about. Then read a book together. Talk about its main idea.

Name_____

Pick a word from the box to finish each sentence.
Write the word on the line.

| afraid   so   surprise   worry |

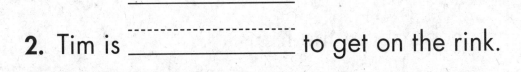

1. Mom has a _____ for Tim.

2. Tim is _____ to get on the rink.

3. Tim does not have to _____ .

4. Mom is _____ quick.
She can help.

Write the answer on the line.

5. Where did Tim use his **surprise?** _____

Home Activity This page helps your child learn to read and write the words *afraid, so, surprise,* and *worry.*
Work through the items with your child. Ask your child to use each word in a sentence.

Name_____

Think about going on
a trip on this ship.
Write about where
you will go.

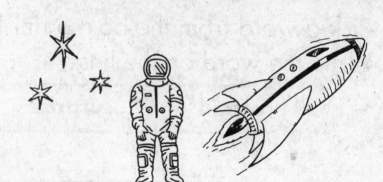

1. Write an ending for the sentence.

_____

On my trip, I will go to _____ .

Write three sentences about the trip.

2. Tell what you will see there.

_____

_____

3. Tell what you will do there.

_____

_____

4. Tell what you like best.

_____

_____

Home Activity This page helps your child practice writing sentences about an imaginary trip. Help your child write the sentences. Then ask your child to write a sentence about the trip home.

© Pearson Education B

Name_____

Read the words.
Circle the word for each picture.

f**o**x

1.	2.	3.	4.

pal pot	sock sack	mop map	bus box

5.	6.	7.	8.

run rock	top tap	fix fox	lock leg

Write a word from the box to finish each sentence.

(hot   mop)

9. Do you see the wet _____?

10. Can I have a _____ drink?

Home Activity This page practices words with the short o sound heard in *fox*. Work through the items with your child. Say each of these short o words, one at a time: *hot, pop, sock, ox*. Ask your child to name words that rhyme with each word.

© Pearson Education B

Name_____

Say the word for each picture.
Write the letters from the box that finish each word.

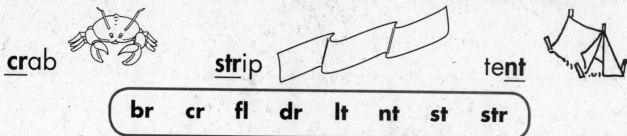

__cr__ab   **str**ip   te**nt**

| br | cr | fl | dr | lt | nt | st | str |

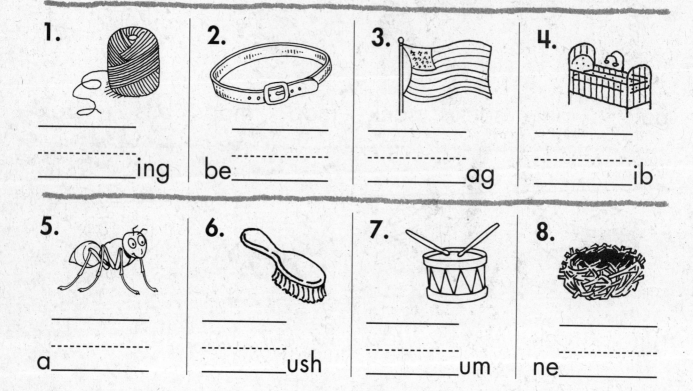

1. _____ing

2. be_____

3. _____ag

4. _____ib

5. a_____

6. _____ush

7. _____um

8. ne_____

Write a sentence using each word.

9. print _____
_____

10. bend _____

Home Activity This page reviews words with consonant blends, as in *crab*, *strip*, and *tent*. Work through the items with your child. Take turns using words with blends in sentences.

12 Phonics Consonant Blends   **Practice Book Unit 1**

© Pearson Education B

Name_____

Read the text.

Answer the questions.

I like frogs. Frogs can do lots of
things. Frogs can live on land and in
ponds. Frogs have long back legs.
They jump and hop with their strong
legs. They can swim too. Frogs see and smell well.
To eat, frogs flick at bugs. They grab the bugs and eat.

1. Write a sentence. Tell what the text is all about.

_____

- -

_____

Circle the word that answers each question.

2. What can frogs eat?

bugs   cats

3. Which tells about frog legs?

fat   strong

4. What is a good name for the text?

Stop and Hop   About Frogs

Home Activity Your child identifies the main idea and details in a paragraph. Work through the items with your child. Together, look at a picture of an animal or observe a real animal. Talk about what the animal looks like and does.

Name_____

Look at the picture and read the sentence.
Pick a word from the box to finish the next sentence.
Write the word on the line.

answer	different	ever	learn

1. Did it ring?

_____

Jack will _____ it.

2. Did you see the fox?

_____

If I _____ see it, I will tell you.

3. Is this truck like that one?

_____

I can see they are _____.

4. Can you spin?

_____

Not yet, but I will _____.

Home Activity This page helps your child read and write the words *answer, different, ever,* and *learn.*
Work through the items with your child. Ask your child to use the words as he or she tells you about the school day.

© Pearson Education B

Name_____

Write names of animals that live in the woods in the web.

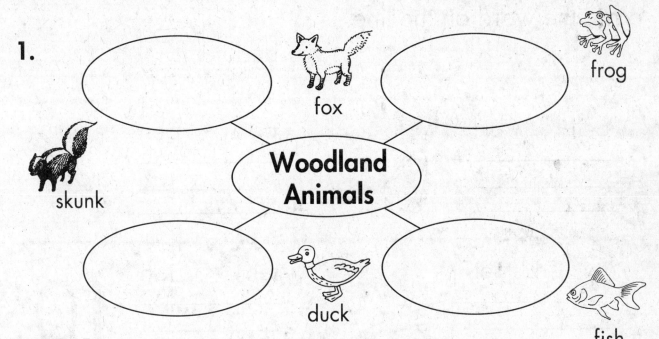

Write one sentence to tell about each animal.

2. _____

3. _____

4. _____

5. _____

Home Activity This page helps your child practice writing sentences about animals. Help your child write the sentences. Together, learn more about one of the animals.

Name_____

Circle the word for each picture.
Write the word on the line.

b<u>e</u>d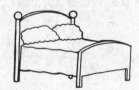

---

bell   bill

1. _____

pan   pen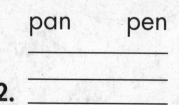

2. _____

---

jot   jet

3. _____

ten   tan

4. _____

10

---

net   not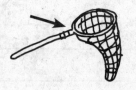

5. _____

tint   tent

6. _____

---

well   will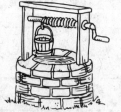

7. _____

disk   desk

8. _____

---

leg   log

9. _____

win   web

10. _____

School + Home

Home Activity This page practices words with the short *e* sound heard in *bed*. Review the items with your child. Together, look through a book or magazine for words that have the short *e* sound as in *bed*.

Name_____

Add -s to each word in the box.
Write the word for each picture.

bed	bug	fan	hop
kick	run	spin	tent

sit**s**

egg**s**

1.

_____

- - - - - - - - - - - - -

_____

2.

_____

- - - - - - - - - - - - -

_____

3.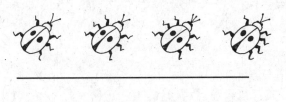

_____

- - - - - - - - - - - - -

_____

4.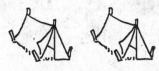

_____

- - - - - - - - - - - - -

_____

5.

_____

- - - - - - - - - - - - -

_____

6.

_____

- - - - - - - - - - - - -

_____

7.

_____

- - - - - - - - - - - - -

_____

8.

_____

- - - - - - - - - - - - -

_____

© Pearson Education B

School + Home **Home Activity** The lesson practices adding the ending -s to verbs and forming plural nouns by adding -s. Review the items with your child. Have your child copy these words and add s to each one: *cut, drink, flag, shop, sled, tub.* Then use the words in sentences.

Name_____

Read the story. **Answer** the questions.

Jen asks Mom and Dad for sand. Mom has a big tub. Dad gets bags of sand. He spills sand in the tub. Mom helps him fill the tub. Now Jen can dig in the sand.

1. **Circle** the sentence that tells what the story is all about.
   Jen gets a tub of sand.
   Sand spills out of the tub.

2. **Write** a detail that tells about the main idea.
   _____
   -
   _____

3. **Write** a title for the story.
   _____
   -
   _____

4. **Write** a sentence. What can Jen do with the sand?
   _____
   -
   _____

Home Activity Your child identifies the main idea and details in a story. Review the items with your child. Tell your child a story about something you have done. Together, think of a good title for your story.

© Pearson Education B

Name_____

Pick a word from the box to match each clue.
Write the word on the line.

> draw   eye   picture   read

1.

_____

- - - - - - - - - - - - - - - - - -

_____

2.

_____

- - - - - - - - - - - - - - - - - -

_____

3.

_____

- - - - - - - - - - - - - - - - - -

_____

4.

_____

- - - - - - - - - - - - - - - - - -

_____

Find the word that best completes the sentence.
Mark the ⬭ to show your answer.

5. I can ___ a cat.
- ⬭ draw
- ⬭ read
- ⬭ eye

6. I like this ___ best.
- ⬭ picture
- ⬭ read
- ⬭ draw

Home Activity This page helps your child read and write the words *draw, eye, picture,* and *read.* Review the items with your child. Make a "word file" box for your child. Provide cards to write and illustrate new words. Add the word cards to the box.

Name_____

Write a word to complete each sentence.
Use words from the box.

| fox | hot | plants | sand |

1. It gets _____ here.

2. The _____ are big and little.

3. Rocks and _____ are on the land.

4. The _____ runs fast.

5. **Write** a sentence. Tell about a desert.

_____

_____

_____

Home Activity This page allows your child to read and write sentences about the desert. Review the sentences with your child. Then look at pictures of deserts, and use sentences to tell each other what you see.

© Pearson Education B

Name_____

Pick a word from the box to match each picture or clue.
Write the word on the line.

duck	bus	cub	drum
cup	truck	sun	bug

p<u>u</u>p

1.

_____

2.

_____

3.

_____

4.

_____

5.

_____

6.

_____

7.

_____

8.

_____

School + Home

Home Activity This page practices words with the short *u* sound heard in *pup*. Review the items with your child. Have your child say a word that rhymes with these short *u* words, *cub* and *sun*. Help your child write each pair of rhyming words.

Name_____

Circle the word for each picture.
Write the word on the line.

shed   fi**sh**   **th**ink   ma**th**

---

1. deck   dish

_____

- - - - - - - - - -

_____

2. thick   slick

_____

- - - - - - - - - -

_____

---

3. pin   thin

_____

- - - - - - - - - -

_____

4. trip   ship

_____

- - - - - - - - - -

_____

---

5. bath   bank

_____

- - - - - - - - - -

_____

6. shell   bell

_____

- - - - - - - - - -

_____

---

7. brush   best

_____

- - - - - - - - - -

_____

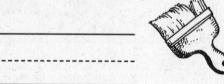

8. pick   path

_____

- - - - - - - - - -

_____

© Pearson Education B

School +Home

Home Activity This page practices words that begin and end with *sh* and *th* as in *shed, fish, think,* and *math.* Review the items with your child. Ask your child to use each word he or she wrote in a sentence that tells about the picture.

Name_____

Read the table.

Write the answer to each question.

Class Pets

Name	Pet
Nat, Beth, Tom	dog
Lin, Jan, Pam, Jim	cat
Will	fish
Josh, Ann	other pets

1. What does this tell about?

_____

- -

_____

2. Sam has a pet like the one Tom has.

_____

What pet does Sam have? _____

3. Does Beth or Will have a big pet? _____

4. Who has a pet with fins? _____

5. What is the pet that 4 people have? _____

© Pearson Education B

School + Home **Home Activity** This page practices how to read a table and draw conclusions. Review the items with your child. Ask your child other questions based on the information in the chart.

Name_____

Pick a word from the box to finish each sentence.
Write the word on the line.

also	among	early	today

1. _____ Beth went to the pond.

2. She got there _____, not late.

3. She saw a frog swim _____ the fish there.

4. She _____ saw ducks swim.

Write a sentence using the word **today**.

5. _____

Home Activity This page helps your child read and write the words *also*, *among*, *early*, and *today*. Review the items with your child. For practice, have your child read each word in the box and use it in a sentence.

Name_____

Circle a topic to complete the sentence.
Write the topic on the line.

_____

1. I want to know about _____ .

pets   trucks   ships

Complete the sentence. Tell who you can ask about your topic.

_____

2. I can ask _____ .

Write three things you know about it.

3. _____

4. _____

5. _____

© Pearson Education B

Home Activity This page helps your child practice choosing a topic and writing sentences about it. Review the items with your child. Then talk about the topic with your child. Together, write another sentence about it.

Name_____

Circle a word to finish each sentence.
Write the word on the line.

 **ch**in
 pa**tch**
wheat

hats   hatch

_____

1. The egg will _____ .

chick   thick

_____

2. The _____ has yellow fuzz.

Ten   When

_____

3. _____ will the bus get here?

Wish   Which

_____

4. _____ one do you like best?

bench   bent

_____

5. We sat on the _____ .

 School + Home   **Home Activity** This page practices words with the sounds of *ch*, *tch*, and *wh*. Review the items with your child. Then ask your child to find something *white* and a *chair* and to tell you the beginning sound of the words. Also ask your child to tell you the ending sound of the word *switch*.

Name_____

lift**ing**

read**ing**

swing**ing**

Use the word in ( ) to finish each sentence.
Add -ing to make a word.
Write the new word on the line.

1. They are _____ to school. (go)

2. Jen is _____ with them. (stand)

3. She is _____ them to stop. (tell)

4. She is _____ to see if they can go. (check)

5. The school bell is _____ . (ring)

Home Activity The activity uses words that end with -ing, such as *lifting* and *drinking*. Say and write a verb, such as *pack, list,* or *fish*. Ask your child to add -ing to it.

Practice Book Unit 2

Phonics Ending -ing **27**

Name_____

Read the story. Then look at the sentences.
Underline clue words such as **next, then,** and **last.**
Write 1, 2, 3, 4, 5 to show the right order.

Mom and I went to the pond to see the ducks. Next, we sat down on a log, and I took out a snack. Then I fed the ducks. Soon, I had none of my snack left. At last, we went back to the van.

_____ At last, we went back to the van.

_____ Soon, I had none of my snack left.

_____ Next, we sat down on a log, and I took out a snack.

_____ Then I fed the ducks.

_____ Mom and I went to the pond to see the ducks.

School + Home

Home Activity Your child numbered events to show sequence. Tell a story, such as "The Three Little Pigs" to your child. Then name three story events and ask your child to tell which happened first, second, and last.

© Pearson Education B

Name_____

Pick a word from the box to finish each sentence.
Write it on the line.

around   eight   enough   nothing

1. I can see _____ cats.

2. The cats have _____ to eat.

3. They look _____ for milk.

4. Now they have _____ to eat.

Pick a word to match each clue.
Mark the ⬭ to show your answer.

5. two plus six
   - ⬭ nothing
   - ⬭ around
   - ⬭ eight

6. none
   - ⬭ around
   - ⬭ enough
   - ⬭ nothing

Home Activity This page helps your child learn to read and write the words *around*, *eight*, *enough*, and *nothing*. Review the items with your child. For practice, give your child a clue for each word and have him or her say the word.

Finish each sentence. **Write** the words on the lines.
The words in the box may help you.

back	drill	fast	truck

1. This is a _____ . The bell rings and rings.

2. We must get out of the school _____ .

3. We see the big red _____.

4. Soon we can go _____ in the school.

5. **Write** a sentence about a drill.

_____

_____

_____

_____

© Pearson Education B

Name_____

Pick a word from the box to finish each sentence.
Write the new word on the line.

| dumped   handed   stacked |

1. Rick _____ the blocks out of the box.

2. Beth _____ the blocks.

3. Ann _____ the blocks to Beth.

Pick a word that completes the sentence.
Mark the ⬭ to show your answer.

4. Rick ____ the blocks out.
   - ⬭ jumped
   - ⬭ yelled
   - ⬭ spilled

5. Beth ____ blocks to the stack.
   - ⬭ added
   - ⬭ brushed
   - ⬭ planted

6. Ann ____ Rick to find some green blocks.
   - ⬭ spelled
   - ⬭ asked
   - ⬭ ended

7. Ann ____ up the last block and gave it to Beth.
   - ⬭ picked
   - ⬭ asked
   - ⬭ ended

© Pearson Education B

Home Activity This activity uses words that end with *-ed*, such as *played* and *jumped*. Choose a word with *-ed* and ask your child to use the word in a sentence.

skip**ping**   run**ning**   clap**ped**   bat**ted**

stopping	hugged	hugging
stopped	sipping	sipped

Double the last letter in each word. **Add -ing** or **-ed** to each word. **Write** the new word on the line.

Add -ed	**Add -ing**
stop **1.** _____	**2.** _____
hug **3.** _____	**4.** _____
sip **5.** _____	**6.** _____

Pick a word from the box to finish each sentence.

7. I am _____ my pet.

8. I _____ a cold drink.

Home Activity The lesson practices adding the ending -ing or -ed to words, such as tap and tag. For these and many other short vowel words, we double the final letter before adding -ed or -ing. Say one of these words: flip, sag, pin. Help your child add -ing and -ed to these words and say the new words.

Name _____

Read the story. **Look** at the pictures.
Write 1, 2, 3, 4 to show the right order.

I tossed the stick. Max was running fast. I did not think
he could get it. Then Max jumped up and grabbed it.
Max ran back to me and dropped the stick.

5. Write a sentence that tells what might happen next.

_____

_____

_____

Home Activity The page practices identifying the sequence of events in a story. With your child, draw pictures showing events in a story. Mix the pictures and have your child put them in order and retell the story.

© Pearson Education B

Name_____

Pick a word from the box to finish each sentence.
Write the word on the line.

| build carry heavy water |

1. The pigs will _____ with bricks.

2. Add _____ and mix it up.

3. We can _____ the bricks and mix in this.

4. They are very _____ .

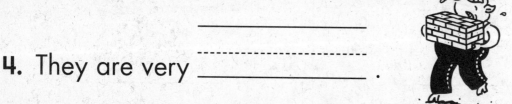

Pick a word from the box to match each clue.
Write the word on the line.

5. You can drink this.

6. to bring with you

_____

_____

Home Activity This page helps your child learn to read and write the words *build, carry, heavy,* and *water.* Review the items with your child. For practice, have your child make up a story using all the words.

© Pearson Education B

Name_____

Choose words from the box.
Finish the sentences.

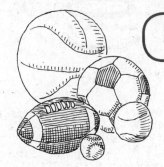

| best   friends   jump   pitch   run   win |

_____

1. I will _____, and he will catch.

_____

2. We did our _____, but we did not win.

Write three sentences about teams.
You can use words from the box.

3. _____

4. _____

5. _____

Home Activity This page helps your child write sentences. Ask your child to talk about team activities and their rules.

Read the words. **Circle** the word for each picture.
Write the word on the line.

v<u>a</u>s<u>e</u>

sn<u>a</u>k<u>e</u>

c<u>a</u>k<u>e</u>

---

1. lake   lack

_____

2. plant   plate

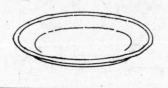

_____

3. tape   tap

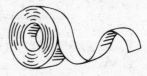

_____

---

4. can   cane

_____

5. mane   man

_____

6. plane   plan

_____

Find a word from the list that rhymes with the first word.
Mark the ⬭ to show your answer.

7. cake
  ⬭ rack
  ⬭ rate
  ⬭ rake

8. cane
  ⬭ lane
  ⬭ clan
  ⬭ can

9. lake
  ⬭ mate
  ⬭ make
  ⬭ man

10. skate
  ⬭ lane
  ⬭ last
  ⬭ late

© Pearson Education B

School + Home **Home Activity** This page practices words that have the long *a* sound as in *vase*. Write *tap, mad, can,* and *cap* on a sheet of paper. Point out that these words have a short *a* sound. Have your child add the final *e* to make new words with the long *a* sound.

Name_____

Pick a word from the box to finish each sentence.
Write the word on the line.

> pace   place   lace   face   page   stage   cage

1. Grace and Kate sing on _____ .

2. Grace has on a white _____ dress.

3. Next to Grace there is a _____ .

4. Oh, no! Kate left a _____ on her desk.

5. Grace finds the _____ on the page for Kate.

6. They sing at a fast _____ .

7. Kate has a grin on her _____ .
   "Thank you, Grace."

Home Activity The lesson reviews words that contain the /s/ sound spelled c as in lace and the /j/ sound spelled g as in cage. Ask your child to think of words that rhyme with these words. Help your child list the words and use them in a sentence.

Name_____

Read the story. **Look** at the pictures. **Write 1, 2, 3, 4** to show the right order.

Today was odd. I took a bag. Then I raced to the bus. At lunch, I looked in the bag. It was not my lunch. It was a bunch of stuff! Dave saw my face and came over. He gave me some of his lunch.

1.

_____

2.

_____

3.

_____

4.

_____

5. Write a sentence that tells what might happen next.

_____

_____

_____

School + Home

Home Activity The page identifies the sequence of events in a story about sharing. Have your child write what he or she would do if a friend forgot a lunch.

Name_____

Pick a word from the box to finish each sentence.
Write it on the line.

┌─────────────────────────────────────┐
│   another   enjoy   few   toward   │
└─────────────────────────────────────┘

1. I _____ picking grapes.

2. I think I will eat _____ one.

3. Would you like a _____ grapes?

4. Two grapes are coming _____ you now!

5. Do you know _____ way to eat them?

Pick a word to match each clue.
Mark the ⬭ to show your answer.

6. not many
   - ⬭ enjoy
   - ⬭ few
   - ⬭ toward

7. adding one
   - ⬭ toward
   - ⬭ around
   - ⬭ another

© Pearson Education B

Home Activity This page helps your child learn to read and write the words *another, enjoy, few,* and *toward.* Work through the items with your child. For practice, have your child use each word in a sentence.

Read the first sentence. How do you share at school?
Write five sentences telling about it.
The words in the box may help you.

| classmates | ball | get in line |
| teacher | play | at math time |

In school I share in many ways.

1. I share the _____ when we play.

2. I share _____ .

3. _____

4. _____

5. _____

School + Home **Home Activity** This page helps your child finish sentences and learn to write sentences. Think about other times your child shares. Help your child write a sentence about one of them.

40 **Writing**

Practice Book Unit 2

© Pearson Education B

Name_____

Read the words. **Circle** the word for each picture.
Write the word on the line.

f<u>i</u>v<u>e</u>

f<u>i</u>r<u>e</u>

k<u>i</u>t<u>e</u>

1. miss   mice

_____

2. bike   big

_____

3. lid   lime

_____

4. pin   pine

_____

5. chin   chime

_____

6. dim   dime

_____

Find the word that rhymes with the picture.
Mark the ⬭ to show your answer.

7. ⬭ rink
⬭ ride
⬭ ripe

8. ⬭ link
⬭ five
⬭ mine

School + Home **Home Activity** This page practices words that have the long *i* sound as in *kite*. Write *hid, rid, bit,* and *kit* on a sheet of paper. These words have a short *i* sound. Have your child add the final *e* and read each new word. Then take turns giving sentences with the new words.

Practice Book Unit 2   **Phonics** Long *i* (CVCe)   **41**

Use the word in ( ) to finish each sentence. **Add -ed** or **-ing** to make a word. Remember to drop the **e**. **Write** the new word on the line.

1. Dad was _____ lunch. (make)

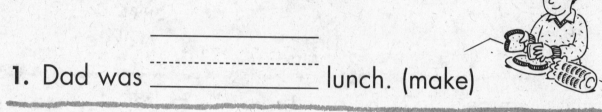

2. He saw Rob _____ toward him. (come)

3. Dad was glad to see Rob.

He _____ . (wave)

4. "I was _____ to see you!" said Dad. (hope)

5. "I like _____ what you make!" said Rob. (taste)

© Pearson Education B

Home Activity This page uses words that end in -ed or -ing, such as *waved* and *smiling*. Have your child add -ed or -ing to these words: *hike, name, skate, drive*. Remind them to drop the e before adding the ending.

Name_____

Read the story. **Answer** the questions.

Many people like games. There are games that use pictures. There are space games. There are games that tell you what to do and how to win. Some games make you go back and do the steps again. Some games have you hiking over the hills. Some have you biking around a track. We can find many games that people like.

1. Which word tells what many people like?

       space   games

2. Which word tells what games can use?

       lines   pictures

3. Write the sentence that tells the main idea.

_____

- -

_____

4. What do some games make you do?
- ⬭ run
- ⬭ hike
- ⬭ eat

5. What do you have to do in some games?
- ⬭ do the steps again
- ⬭ ride in trucks
- ⬭ hop up and down

© Pearson Education B

Home Activity This page works with the main idea and supporting details in a story. Tell a story about toys your child likes to play with. Have your child identify the main idea and details in this story.

Name_____

Circle the word that matches each clue.

1. look up to see it   moon   through

2. I'm done. I'm ___.   instead   through

3. Go there. Go ___ the lake.   moon   across

4. in place of   through   instead

Pick a word from the box to finish each sentence.
Write the word on the line.

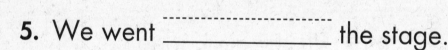

| across   instead   Moon   through |

5. We went _____ the stage.

6. We sang "I See the _____ ."

7. We went _____ it two times.

8. Next, we sang about the sun _____ of
   the moon.

School + Home   **Home Activity** This page helps your child learn to read and write the words *across, instead, moon,* and *through*. Work through the items with your child. For practice, have your child create new sentences using the words.

Name_____

Read about how ants work together.

Ants live together. Every ant has a job. One ant helps the little ants. One ant fixes things. One takes out the trash. Ants like to work together.

How are ants like a family? **Write** 5 sentences.

1. Ants are like a family. Every ant has a job.

_____

In a family, _____

_____

2. _____

_____

3. _____

_____

4. _____

_____

5. _____

© Pearson Education B

Home Activity This page helps your child finish and write sentences. Discuss how ants and people are alike. Then discuss how they are different. Make a chart to show these similarities and differences.

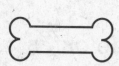  

b<u>o</u>n<u>e</u>　　　　　st<u>ove</u>　　　　　h<u>o</u>s<u>e</u>

Read the words. **Circle** the word for each picture.
Write the word on the line.

1. not　note	2. nod　nose	3. rose　rob
	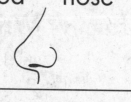	
_____	_____	_____

4. rod　rode	5. home　hot	6. globe　got

_____	_____	_____

Find the word that rhymes with the picture.
Mark the ⬭ to show your answer.

7. ⬭ bone
　 ⬭ kite
　 ⬭ cake

8. ⬭ cape
　 ⬭ hope
　 ⬭ dime

 Home Activity This page practices words that have the long o sound as in *bone*. Write *not* on an index card. Have your child add a final *e* to make *note*. Write *note* on the other side of the card. Then have your child make a sentence using both words. Do the same for *hop/hope* and *rod/rode*.

Name_____

Circle a word to finish each sentence.
Write the word on the line.

1 cat**'s** food   2 cat**s'** food

dog's   dogs'
_____
- - - - - - - - - - - -

1. This is the _____ bone.

cat's   cats'
_____
- - - - - - - - - - - -

2. This is the _____ milk.

twins'   twin's
_____
- - - - - - - - - - - -

3. The _____ box is for the cat.

pets'   pet's
_____
- - - - - - - - - - - -

4. The _____ boxes are little.

dog's   dogs'
_____
- - - - - - - - - - - -

5. The _____ box is little.

© Pearson Education B

Home Activity This page shows how to form the possessive of singular and plural nouns. Write each pair of words on paper: *teacher's, teachers'; student's, students'; brother's, brothers'; sister's, sisters'.* Help your child use each word in a sentence.

Name_____

Read the story. **Write** your answers on the lines.
Write complete sentences.

My name is Len. I have a friend named Tad.
He writes about dogs. He is so good that he
got a prize. I wanted to make a picture for
Tad. I made a big dog. I put "Way to go!"
by the picture. Tad liked my dog picture.

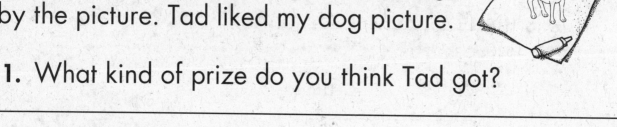

1. What kind of prize do you think Tad got?

_____
- -
_____

2. Why did Len draw a dog?

_____
- -
_____

Read the questions. **Mark** the ⬭ to show your answer.

3. What did Len think
when Tad got a prize?
- ⬭ Len was glad.
- ⬭ Len was mad.
- ⬭ Len was sad.

4. What does Tad think of
Len?
- ⬭ He is talented.
- ⬭ He is not talented.
- ⬭ He does not like him.

© Pearson Education B

Home Activity This page practices drawing conclusions about a story. Work with your child to make a picture. Decide together to whom you should give the picture. Ask your child to explain (draw conclusions about) why that person should get the picture.

Name_____

Pick a word from the box to finish each sentence. **Write** the word on the line.

| father | mother | remember | touch |

1. I _____ the fun we had when I was little.

2. My _____ would sing. We had to do what he said.

3. I would _____ my hand and then my leg!

4. My _____ did the same. She looked surprised.

Pick a word from the box to match each clue.
Write the word on the line.

5. dad _____

6. to pat _____

7. mom _____

8. to think about _____

School + Home **Home Activity** This page helps your child learn to read and write the words *father, mother, remember,* and *touch.* Work through the items with your child. For practice, have your child tell a story using all the words.

Practice Book Unit 2

High-Frequency Words 49

© Pearson Education B

Name_____

Pretend you are having a party.
Make a "to do" list like this one.

to do:
☐ make a cake
☐ pick up things
☐ take bath
☐ get dressed

Write five sentences from your list.

1. Today people will come over.
_____

First, I will -
_____ .
_____

2. Then I will - .
_____

3. - .
_____

4. - .
_____

5. - .
_____

© Pearson Education B

Home Activity This page helps your child finish and write sentences. Think about celebrations you have had. Help your child write about preparing for the special day.

Name_____

Circle a word to finish each sentence.
Write the word on the line.

c**u**b**e**   Z**e**k**e**

---

flute   frame

_____

1. Fen has a drum and a _____ .

Pete   Penny

_____

2. _____ comes to see Fen.

---

ace   use

_____

3. "Can I _____ one?" he asks.

---

these   tame

_____

4. "Which of _____ would you like?" asks Fen.

---

tune   tame

_____

5. The two of them make a nice _____ .

School + Home **Home Activity** This page practices words with the *u* sound heard in *cube* and the *e* sound heard in *Zeke*. Work through the items with your child. Then help your child write these words and tell what they mean: *rule, eve, cute, theme.*

Name_____

Write the contraction that is formed from each pair of words on the line. **Use** the words in the box.

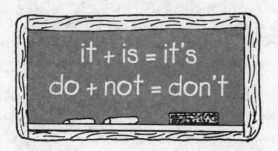

it + is = it's
do + not = don't

hasn't	who's
that's	what's
won't	couldn't

1. could not

_____

- - - - - - - - - - - - -

_____

2. that is

_____

- - - - - - - - - - - - -

_____

3. has not

_____

- - - - - - - - - - - - -

_____

4. who is

_____

- - - - - - - - - - - - -

_____

5. what is

_____

- - - - - - - - - - - - -

_____

6. will not

_____

- - - - - - - - - - - - -

_____

Pick a word from the box to finish each sentence. **Write** the word on the line.

she's	isn't

7. Pam _____ done yet.

8. You can see that _____ still building.

Home Activity This page reviews contractions such as *it's* and *couldn't*. Work through the items with your child. Write each contraction from this page on cards. Hold up a card and ask your child to tell what two words were used to form the contraction.

Name_____

Read the story. **Ask** yourself what is happening.

Answer each question.

The bell rings at eight.
The kids line up.
Miss Hanks takes them
to class. The kids sit at
desks. They learn lots of new things today. They eat
lunch. At last, the bell rings at three.

1. Where are the kids? _____

_____

2. Who is Miss Hanks? _____

3. What kinds of things could the kids learn?

_____

_____

4. **Draw** a picture of what
could take place next.
Write a sentence to
tell about it.

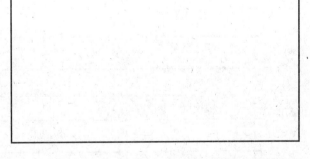

_____

_____

Home Activity Your child reads a story and draws conclusions from the information in the story and the
illustration. Work through the items with your child. Talk about what else might happen during the school day.

Name_____

Pick a word from the box
to match each clue.
Write the word on the line.

| house | idea |
| machine | sign |

1.

_____
\- - - - - - - - - - - - - - - - -
_____

2.

_____
\- - - - - - - - - - - - - - - - -
_____

---

3. It does work
for people.

_____
\- - - - - - - - - - - - - - - - -
_____

4. You can
think of this.

_____
\- - - - - - - - - - - - - - - - -
_____

Write a sentence for each word in the box.

5. _____

6. _____

7. _____

8. _____

Home Activity This page helps your child read and write the words *house, idea, machine,* and *sign.* Work through the items with your child. Assist your child in creating a "Helpful Words" dictionary that contains each word, a written definition, and a picture when appropriate.

© Pearson Education B

Name_____

Think of four things you would like to make.
List your ideas in the web.

1.

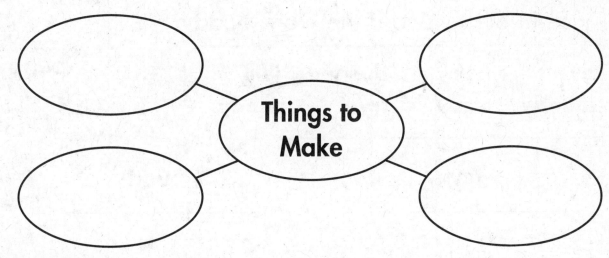

Things to Make

Complete each sentence.
Write about something you would like to make.
Write the steps you would use to make it.

2. I would like to make _____ .

3. First, _____ .

4. Next, _____ .

5. Last, _____ .

School + Home

Home Activity This page helps your child practice writing sentences about an invention he or she would like to make. Help your child write the sentences. Ask your child to draw and label the invention described on this page.

© Pearson Education B

Name_____

Read each word in the box.
Write the words that have the vowel
sound of **y** as in **my** under the word **my**.
Write the words that have the vowel sound
of **y** as in **buddy** under the word **buddy**.

fl**y**

pupp**y**

| by | dry | dusty | jelly |
| muddy | spy | try | windy |

my	**buddy**
1. _____	5. _____
2. _____	6. _____
3. _____	7. _____
4. _____	8. _____

Find the word that has the same ending sound as the
picture. **Mark** the space to show your answer.

9. ⬯ hasn't
   ⬯ hobby
   ⬯ hunted

10. ⬯ why
    ⬯ we
    ⬯ was

Home Activity This page practices words with the vowel sounds of y as in *fly* and *puppy*. Work through the items with your child. Together, make a list of words that end with the two vowel sounds of y.

56 Phonics Vowel Sounds of *y*

Practice Book Unit 3

© Pearson Education B

Name_____

 watch**es**   stud**ies**  box**es**  fli**es**

Use the word in ( ) to finish each sentence.
Add -es or **change** the **y** to **i** and **add -es** to make a word.
Write the new word on the line.

1. Jade _____ the mats. (carry)

2. Mom stacks the _____ . (dish)

3. Jan gets the _____ . (glass)

4. Dad _____ on some grapes and helps. (munch)

5. Luz _____ the things. (dry)

 Home Activity This page practices words with the ending *-es* as in *watches* and the plural *-es* as in *boxes*. Work through the items with your child. Have your child write the following words and add *-es* or change the *y* to *i* and add *-es* to each word: *buzz, sky, toss, penny, patch, bus.*

Name_____

Read each character's words and **look** at each picture.
Pick a word from the box that tells how the character
feels. **Write** the word on the line.

> brave   dizzy   happy   sad   surprised

1. Hank looks for his
   dog. He can't find her. _____

2. Rin spins and spins on her
   skates. She must close her eyes. _____

3. Sam wins the
   game. He gets a prize. _____

4. Eve looks behind the
   bed. Her pet hops out. _____

© Pearson Education B

5. A cat is stuck on a
   branch. Bly saves the cat. _____

School + Home

Home Activity The activity practices drawing conclusions from the characters' words and the illustrations.
Work through the items with your child. Then read a story together and draw conclusions using the words
and pictures.

Name_____

Pick a word from the box to finish each sentence.
Write the word on the line.

against	found	stood	wild

1. The game was the Ducks _____ the Flames.

2. Ben had a _____ idea.

3. He went and _____ a buddy.

4. They _____ up and spelled out "GO!"

5. What was Ben's wild idea? **Write** a sentence to tell about it.

_____

_____

_____

Home Activity This page helps your child learn to read and write the words *against*, *found*, *stood*, and *wild*. Work through the items with your child. Ask your child to retell the story on this page, using each of the words from the box.

Name_____

Write four sentences that tell about different ways people tell things to others.
The words in the box may help you.

answer	picture	told	note
machine	code	sign	

1. _____

2. _____

3. _____

4. _____

5. **Write** an answer to the question.
   How do you like to tell things to others?

_____

_____

_____

School + Home

Home Activity This page helps your child write sentences about ways that people talk with each other. Together, write a letter or an e-mail to a friend or family member.

60 Writing   **Practice Book Unit 3**

Name_____

| dark | jar | sharp |
| hard | chart | starts |

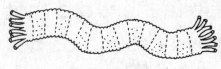

sc**ar**f

Write the word from the box that rhymes with each word below.

1. park

_____

_____

2. car

_____

_____

3. cart

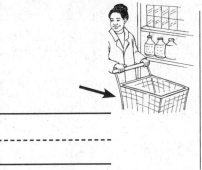

_____

_____

4. card

_____

_____

Pick a word from the box that is the opposite of each word below. Write the word on the line.

5. dull

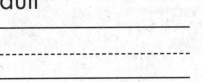

_____

_____

6. stops

_____

_____

© Pearson Education B

Name_____

Circle the word that has the same vowel sound as **born**.
Write the word on the line.

c**or**n   sh**ore**

1.

_____

- - - - - - - - - - -

_____

dish   fork

2.

_____

- - - - - - - - - - -

_____

pit   core

3.

_____

- - - - - - - - - - -

_____

store   cart

4.

_____

- - - - - - - - - - -

_____

horn   drum

5.

_____

- - - - - - - - - - -

_____

sun   storm

6.

_____

- - - - - - - - - - -

_____

cord   rope

Write a sentence using the word.

7. more

_____

- -

_____.

Home Activity This page practices words with the vowel sound in *corn* and *shore*. Work through the items with your child. Ask your child to name words that rhyme with *corn* or *shore*. Write the words and read the list together.

© Pearson Education B

Name_____

Read the stories. **Follow** the directions below.

Mike wants to get to school early.
He sets his clock to wake his dog,
Spot. Spot licks Mike's hand. Mike
gets up. He takes the early bus.

1. Write the sentence that tells what the story is all about.

_____
- -
_____ .

2. Underline the sentences that tell the details of the story.

Kim gets string and two sticks. She
gets more things. She adds the sticks
and string. Kim makes a kite.

3. Write the sentence that tells what the story is about.

_____
- -
_____ .

4. Underline the sentences that tell the details of the story.

5. Write a good title for each of these stories.

_____
- -
_____

Home Activity This page helps your child identify the main idea and details in stories. Work through the items with your child. Then read a book together. Talk about the main idea.

Name_____

Look at each picture.
Pick a word from the box to finish each sentence.
Write the word on the line.

| become   even   front   thought |

1. This block would _____ Bill's car.

2. Bill _____ he could make the best car.

3. Dad put heavy parts on

the _____ and back of the car.

4. Bill's car could _____ win.

Write the answers on the lines.

5. What would the block become? _____

6. What thought did Bill have?

_____

_____

© Pearson Education B

School + Home

Home Activity This page helps your child learn to read and write the words *become*, *even*, *front*, and *thought*. Work through the items with your child. Ask your child to use each word in the box in a sentence.

Name_____

Complete the chart.
Write three ways that ideas can be good.
Write three ways that ideas can be bad.

Ideas

Good	Bad
1. _____	4. _____
2. _____	5. _____
3. _____	6. _____

Complete each sentence.
Use some of your ideas from the chart.

7. Ideas are good when

_____

_____ .

8. Ideas are bad when

_____

_____ .

© Pearson Education B

Name_____

Pick a word from the box to name each picture.
Write the word on the line.

ki**tte**n  b**aske**t

button	rabbit	blanket	costume	picnic
puppet	doctor	tadpole	trombone	tunnel

1. _____

2. _____

3. _____

4. _____

5. _____

6. _____

7. _____

8. _____

9. _____

10. _____

© Pearson Education B

School + Home **Home Activity** This page practices words with the VCCV pattern as in *kitten* and *basket*. Work through the items with your child. Have your child write and illustrate each of the following words: *mittens, insect,* and *magnet.*

Name_____

Alma is getting ready to plant a garden. **Look** at the pictures. **Write** the words **first, second, next,** and **last** to show the right order of events.

1.

_____
- - - - - - - - - - - - - - - - - -
_____

2.

_____
- - - - - - - - - - - - - - - - - -
_____

3.

_____
- - - - - - - - - - - - - - - - - -
_____

4.

_____
- - - - - - - - - - - - - - - - - -
_____

5. Write a sentence that tells what might happen next.

_____
- -
_____
- -
_____

School + Home **Home Activity** The activity practices identifying the sequence of steps needed to plant a garden. Work through the items with your child. Together, write the steps your child should take when getting ready for a favorite activity.

Name_____

Pick a word from the box to finish each sentence.
Write the word on the line.

| easy   follow   knew   usual |

1. It was _____ to get to the park.

2. Calvin would _____ the long path.

3. It was his _____ way to go.

4. Betty _____ a quick way to go.

5. Betty would _____ the short path.

6. **Write** an answer to the question.

Who would get to the park fast? _____

Home Activity This page helps your child read and write the words *easy*, *follow*, *knew*, and *usual*. Work through the items with your child. Ask your child to tell how to get from one place to another, using the words in the box.

© Pearson Education B

Name_____

Write about a problem and how you would solve it.

_____

1. Problem: _____

How to Solve the Problem

_____

2. At the start, _____ .

_____

3. Next, _____ .

_____

4. Last, _____ .

Write an answer to the questions.

5. Did you find a good way to solve the problem? Why do you think so?

_____

_____

_____

_____

© Pearson Education B

Home Activity This activity involves identifying a problem and how to solve it. Ask your child to write about another way the problem might have been solved.

Name_____

Write the contraction that is formed from each pair of words on the line.

<u>**I will**</u> make a picture.
<u>**I'll**</u> make a picture.

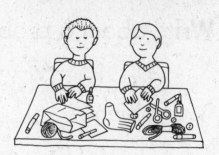

---

1. they will

_____

- - - - - - - - - - - - - - - - - -

_____

2. it will

_____

- - - - - - - - - - - - - - - - - -

_____

---

3. I am

_____

- - - - - - - - - - - - - - - - - -

_____

4. she will

_____

- - - - - - - - - - - - - - - - - -

_____

---

5. you will

_____

- - - - - - - - - - - - - - - - - -

_____

6. he will

_____

- - - - - - - - - - - - - - - - - -

_____

Pick a word from the box to finish each sentence.
Write the word on the line. **Begin** with a capital letter.

> **we'll   it'll**

_____

7. - - - - - - - - - - - - - - - - make puppets.

_____

_____

8. - - - - - - - - - - - - - - - - be fun.

© Pearson Education B

Home Activity This page reviews contractions such as *I'm* and *they'll*. Work through the items with your child. As you read with your child, point out contractions. Ask your child to say the two words used to make each contraction.

Name_____

Read the words. **Circle** the word for each picture.
Write the word on the line.

crack**er**   sh**ir**t   n**ur**se

1. porch   purse

_____

2. skirt   score

_____

3. fern   farm

_____

4. gate   girl

_____

5. lucky   ladder

_____

6. burger   boring

_____

Pick a word that is the opposite of each word below.
Mark the 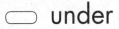 to show your answer.

7. over
   ◯ under
   ◯ every
   ◯ other

8. last
   ◯ dirt
   ◯ first
   ◯ bird

© Pearson Education B

School + Home

Home Activity This page practices words with the vowel sound in *fern, shirt,* and *nurse.* Work through the items with your child. Ask your child to name rhyming words for *skirt* and *turn.*

Read the story. **Underline** clue words such as **first, next, after,** and **last. Write 1, 2, 3** to show the right order.

Marlene is baking a cake. **First,** she mixes things up. **Next,** she puts the cake batter in a pan. **After** that, Marlene puts the pan in to bake. The cake bakes for a long time. Marlene takes the cake out. She lets it sit. At **last,** Marlene puts on the icing.

_____ After that, Marlene puts the pan in to bake.

_____ First, she mixes things up.

_____ Next, she puts the cake batter in a pan.

Which happens after the cake bakes?
- ⬭ Marlene mixes things up.
- ⬭ Marlene takes the cake out.
- ⬭ Marlene puts the cake batter in a pan.

© Pearson Education B

School + Home **Home Activity** Your child identifies words that show sequence and places events in the correct order. Work through the items with your child. Together, write the steps you take when making a favorite food.

Name_____

Pick a word from the box to match each clue.
Write the word on the line.

along	both	color	guess

_____

1. try to think of an answer   _____

2. going on one path   _____

3. red, blue, green, or yellow   _____

4. two together   _____

Write sentences for each word in the box.

5. _____

6. _____

7. _____

8. _____

Home Activity This page helps your child read and write the words *along, both, color,* and *guess.* Work through the items with your child. Make a "word file" box for your child out of a shoebox. Provide scraps of paper or index cards to write and illustrate new words.

Name_____

List four places where ideas come from in the web.

1.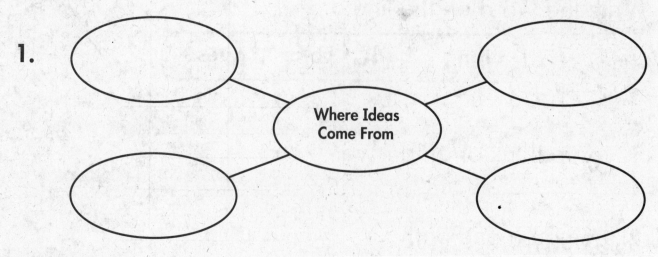

Where Ideas
Come From

Write three sentences that tell about places where ideas come from.

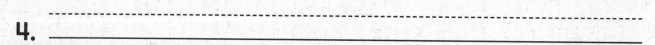

2. _____

_____

3. _____

_____

4. _____

Write an answer to the question.

5. Where do you get your best ideas from?

_____

_____

 Home Activity This page helps your child write sentences about where ideas come from. Review your child's sentences. Talk with your child about places where you get your ideas.

74 Writing

Practice Book Unit 3

© Pearson Education B

Name_____

Circle the word for each picture.
Write the word on the line.

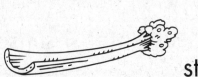 st<u>al</u>k

 f<u>all</u>

1. ball   bill

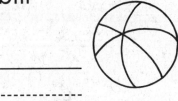

_____

- - - - - - - - - - - - - - -

2. chalk   chick

_____

- - - - - - - - - - - - - - -

3. sat   salt

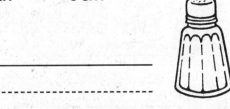

_____

- - - - - - - - - - - - - - -

4. can   call

_____

- - - - - - - - - - - - - - -

Find the word that rhymes with the picture.
Mark the ⬭ to show your answer.

5. ⬭ wake
   ⬭ wall
   ⬭ walk

6. ⬭ talk
   ⬭ take
   ⬭ tall

School + Home   **Home Activity** The page works with words that have the sound of *a* as in *ball* and *walk*. Write *all* and *alk* on paper. Have your child list words that end with these letters. Together, think of a rhyme using those words.

© Pearson Education B

Name_____

Say the word for each picture.
Circle the two words that make this word.
Write the compound word on the line.

sun + set = sunset

1.

base   man   shine   sun

_____
- - - - - - - - - - - - - - - - - -
_____

2.

pan   walk   box   lunch

_____
- - - - - - - - - - - - - - - - - -
_____

3.

pack   cup   desk   back

_____
- - - - - - - - - - - - - - - - - -
_____

4.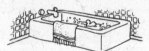

tub   top   cake   bath

_____
- - - - - - - - - - - - - - - - - -
_____

Find the word that you can add to *side* to make a
compound word. **Mark** the ⬭ to show your answer.
Write the word.

5. side _____
   - - - - - - - - - - - - - - - -

   ⬭ mix
   ⬭ walk
   ⬭ ball

6. _____ side
   - - - - - - - - - - - - - - - -

   ⬭ in
   ⬭ sun
   ⬭ chalk

School + Home

Home Activity The page practices compound words. These are words that are made of two smaller
words, such as *sunshine* and *bathmat*. Work with your child to use the words on the page to make up other
compound words: *sunrise, desktop, baseball.*

Name_____

Look for ways in which Tom is **not** like his brother Max.
Write a sentence about Tom. The
words in the box may help you.

| small | big | tall | family | short |

1. _____

Write a sentence that tells how the brothers are alike.

2. _____

Look for ways in which Max is **not** like Tom.
Write a sentence about Max.

3. _____

School + Home **Home Activity** The activity describes ways in which two brothers are alike and different. Talk about how members of your own family are alike and different.

Name_____

Pick a word from the box to match each clue.
Write the word on the line.

| gone group move neighbor promise |

1. not here

_____

- - - - - - - - - - - - - - - -

_____

2. to go to a new place

_____

- - - - - - - - - - - - - - - -

_____

3. He lives near you.

_____

- - - - - - - - - - - - - - - -

_____

4. people together

_____

- - - - - - - - - - - - - - - -

_____

Pick a word from the box to finish each sentence.
Write the word on the line.

5. My _____ Lin lives on my block.

6. She is going to _____ away.

7. I am sad. She will be _____ in no time.

8. Lin said, "I _____ I will write to you!"

Home Activity This page helps your child learn to read and write the words *gone, group, move, neighbor,* and *promise.* Work through the items with your child. For practice, take turns with your child using each word in a sentence.

Name_____

How could you help a friend who is moving away?
Write five sentences about it.
The words in the box may help you.

help	promise	visit
write	miss	call

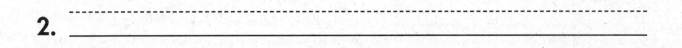

1. I can _____
   put toys in boxes.

2. _____

3. _____

4. _____

5. _____

School + Home **Home Activity** This page helps your child finish sentences and learn to write sentences. Talk about what you and your child can do to help a friend who is moving to another place. Help your child write sentences and draw pictures.

Say the word for each picture.
Write ai or ay to finish the word.

tr**ai**n

tr**ay**

1.

h _____

2.

ch _____ n

3.

p _____ l

4.

spr _____

5.

r _____

6.

n _____ l

7.

br _____ d

8.

sn _____ l

Find the word that rhymes with the picture.
Mark the ⬭ to show your answer.

9. ⬭ pal
   ⬭ pail
   ⬭ pill

10. ⬭ day
    ⬭ dad
    ⬭ trap

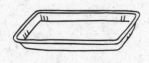

Home Activity This page practices words with the long a sound spelled ai and ay. Work through the items with your child. Then together think of and write five or more words that contain the long a sound spelled ai or ay.

Name_____

Pick a word from the box to finish each sentence.
Write the word on the line.

eat   sweet   tree   teeth   peach   He   seed   be

1. Lee has a _____ in his hand.

2. _____ got it from his yard.

3. There is a peach _____ back there.

4. It gives big, _____ peaches.

5. The _____ of a peach is called a pit.

6. Don't worry! Lee won't _____ the pit.

7. It will _____ easy to find.

8. He'll feel it with his _____ .

Home Activity This page uses words that contain the long *e* sound spelled *e*, *ee*, and *ea*. Ask your child to think of other words that contain the long *e* sound spelled these three ways. Help your child write each word on a card, and then group words that have the same spelling pattern.

Name_____

 peach pit   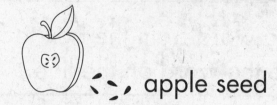 apple seed

Look for ways in which a peach pit is **not** like an apple seed. **Write** a word from the box to finish each sentence.

small   big   peach   apple

1. The peach pit is _____ .

2. The peach pit is inside a _____ .

3. The apple seed is _____ .

4. The apple seed is inside an _____ .

5. Write a sentence that tells how these two things are alike.

_____

_____

_____

_____

© Pearson Education B

 School + Home **Home Activity** The activity has your child describing ways in which two seeds are alike and different. Ask your child to describe differences and similarities in seeds of other familiar fruit, such as oranges, lemons, pears, and plums.

Name_____

Pick a word from the box to finish each sentence. **Write** it on the line.

above	almost	change
often	straight	

1. My green beans are planted in

   _____

   a _____ line.

2. It is _____ time to pick them.

3. Each day I see a _____ in their size.

4. I don't water them too _____ .

5. Enough water falls from _____ .

Pick a word to match each clue. **Mark** the ⬭ to show your answer.

6. many times
   - ⬭ above
   - ⬭ change
   - ⬭ often

7. up high
   - ⬭ straight
   - ⬭ above
   - ⬭ almost

Home Activity This page helps your child learn to read and write the words *above, almost, change, often,* and *straight.* Work through the items with your child. For practice, take turns with your child using each word in a sentence.

© Pearson Education B

Name_____

A. Complete the chart. Write the names of two plants. Write two details about each plant.

_____   _____
- - - - - - - - -   - - - - - - - - -
_____   _____

1. _____   **3.** _____
- - - - - - - - -   - - - - - - - - -
_____   _____

2. _____   **4.** _____

B. Write two sentences to tell how the plants are the same. Write two sentences to tell how the plants are not the same. Use some of your ideas from the chart.

_____
- -
5. _____
_____

- -
6. _____
_____

- -
7. _____
_____

- -
8. _____

Home Activity This page helps your child write sentences. Discuss other plants with your child. Talk about how they are similar and how they are different. Have your child choose two plants, draw pictures of them, and write about them.

Name_____

This cat is **big.**
This dog is **bigger.**
This cow is **biggest.**

This dog is **funny.**
This dog is **funnier.**
This dog is **funniest.**

Circle a word to finish each sentence.
Write the word on the line.

smaller   smallest
_____
- - - - - - - - - - - - -

1. The striped fish is the _____ .

sad   sadder
_____
- - - - - - - - - - - - -

2. Bill is _____ than Gabe.

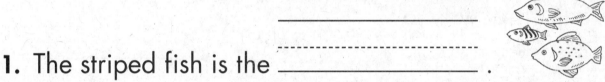

3. These children are happy,

happier   happiest
_____
- - - - - - - - - - - - -
but Sarah is the _____ .

© Pearson Education B

Home Activity This activity uses words that end with -er (higher) and -est (highest) to make comparisons.
Name some animals. Discuss which animal is the fastest, the smallest, and the slowest.

Name_____

Read each sentence. **Circle** the word with the **o** sound as in **goat, go,** and **window. Write** the word on the line.
My g**oa**t will g**o** in the wind**ow**.

1. She came in to get oats.

_____

2. She roamed in the kitchen.

_____

3. She crept way low.

_____

4. That was so Mom would not see.

_____

5. It did her no good.

_____

6. Mom knows all things.

_____

7. "You need to go," Mom said.

_____

8. Flo sadly left our house.

_____

School + Home **Home Activity** The page uses words that have the long *o* sound spelled *o, oa,* and *ow*. Ask your child to draw a picture to go with the story of the goat. Work together to write a sentence about the picture.

Name_____

List two ways a kitten and
a cat are the same. The words
in the box may help you.

kitten   cat

tails   small   big   legs   grown   grow

1. _____

2. _____

List two ways a kitten and a cat are not the same.

3. _____

4. _____

Home Activity Your child describes ways in which two animals are alike and different. Talk with your child about differences and similarities in other animals and their babies, such as rabbits, pigs, ducks, robins, and deer.

© Pearson Education B

Practice Book Unit 4   **Comprehension** Compare and Contrast **87**

Name_____

Circle a word to finish each sentence.
Write the word on the line.

animal   warm

_____

1. I like one farm _____ the best.

animal   field

_____

2. The farm has a _____ with grain.

country   cover

_____

3. My friends like the _____ more than the city.

field   warm

_____

4. Field mice live in holes to keep _____ .

field   cover

_____

5. They run for _____ when they see our cat.

Home Activity This page helps your child learn to read and write the words *animal, country, cover, field,* and *warm.* Work through the items with your child. For practice, have your child make new sentences with the words.

© Pearson Education B

Name_____

Write sentences about a favorite animal. Tell how it changes as it grows. The words in the box may help you.

baby	**lives**	**grows**	**helpless**
take care	**small**	**big**	**eats**

My Favorite Animal

1. I like _____ because _____

_____

2. _____

_____

3. _____

_____

4. _____

_____

5. _____

 Home Activity This page helps your child finish sentences and write new sentences about a favorite animal. Have your child draw pictures of the animal as a baby and as an adult. Have your child tell you more about the animal he or she chose.

Name_____

Read each sentence.
Circle the word with the
i sound as in **pie** and **high**.
Write the word on the line.

That p**ie** is so h**igh**!

1. This is Ned's first night on the job. _____

2. Can he bake ten lemon pies? _____

3. Will they taste all right? _____

4. He tries his best. _____

5. The crust is light and golden. _____

6. Ned's baking turns out just right! _____

© Pearson Education B

School + Home

Home Activity This page practices words with the long *i* sound spelled *ie* and *igh*. Ask your child to create an advertisement for Ned's pies. Use the words *light* and *out of sight*.

90 **Phonics** Long *i: igh, ie*

Read the story. **Circle** a word to **answer** each question.

My dog Gus is part of the family. He
sleeps on my bed. We play together.
He jumps all around. I take him to the
frog pond. Gus is my best pal. Today,
Dad told me Gus is sick. That made
me feel sad. I will help Gus get well.

1. Which word tells a main idea about Gus?
family   bed

2. Which word gives a detail?
play   take

3. Write the sentence that tells the main idea.

_____

- -

_____

- -

_____

4. What is NOT a detail in the story?
⬡ Gus goes to the frog pond.
⬡ Gus jumps all around.
⬡ Gus is sad.

Home Activity This page asks your child to describe the main idea and supporting details in a story about
a girl and her dog. Talk about someone or something your child loves and why. Have your child identify the
main idea and details.

Name_____

Pick a word from the box to match each clue.
Write the word on the line.

> below   child   children   full   important

1. under

_____
- - - - - - - - - - - - - - - -
_____

2. one kid

_____
- - - - - - - - - - - - - - - -

3. no empty space

_____
- - - - - - - - - - - - - - - -
_____

4. two kids

_____
- - - - - - - - - - - - - - - -

Pick a word from the box to finish each sentence.
Write the word on the line.

5. Sofia is my best pal.

She is _____ to me.
- - - - - - - - - - - - - - - -

6. We go to school with

_____
- - - - - - - - - - - - - - - -

many other _____ .

© Pearson Education B

Home Activity This page helps your child learn to read and write the words *below*, *child*, *children*, *full*, and *important*. Work through the items with your child. Then use the words to make up a story about your family with your child. Take turns adding sentences.

Name_____

A. Think about going to a new school. **List** reasons why it is hard. Then list ideas of things you could do to make it easier.

Why it is hard to go to a new school	What I can do to make it easier
1. _____	4. _____
2. _____	5. _____
3. _____	6. _____

B. Write sentences to tell about going to a new school. Tell what is hard and what you can do to help. Use ideas from the chart.

Going to a new school is hard because _____

_____

_____

_____

School + Home **Home Activity** This page helps your child finish sentences and learn to write sentences. Ask your child to describe how he or she would feel in a new school. Talk about ways to adjust to this change.

Name_____

Read the word that is formed from each pair of syllables. 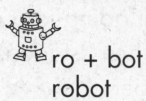 ro + bot **Write** the word on the line. robot

 cab + in cabin

---

1. spi + der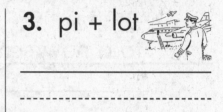

_____

- - - - - - - - - - - - -

_____

2. rob + in

_____

- - - - - - - - - - - - -

_____

3. pi + lot

_____

- - - - - - - - - - - - -

_____

4. lem + on

_____

- - - - - - - - - - - - -

_____

5. mu + sic

_____

- - - - - - - - - - - - -

_____

Pick a word from above to finish each sentence.
Write the word on the line.

6. The _____ landed the plane.

7. I saw a _____ in a web.

8. I saw a _____ in the park.

9. The band played march _____ .

School + Home

Home Activity This page practices words with open syllables (those that end in a vowel) and closed syllables (those that end in a consonant). Write *bacon, medal, salad,* and *paper.* Have your child put a line between the two syllables in each word.

© Pearson Education B

Name_____

Look for ways in which one day is **not** like the other. **Write** one sentence about each day. The words in the box may help you.

cold	snowy	hot	sunny	fun	play

_____

1. _____

_____

2. _____

Write a sentence that tells how Jo Ann dresses when it is hot.

_____

3. _____

Write a sentence that tells how Jo Ann dresses when it is cold.

_____

4. _____

 School + Home

Home Activity The activity describes days with two different types of weather and how a girl dresses for each. Talk with your child about how each of you feel about different types of weather.

Name_____

Circle the word that matches each clue.

1. where your eyes are

head

wash

2. big

poor

large

3. have nothing

large

poor

4. to clean

poor

wash

Pick a word from the box to finish each sentence.
Write the word on the line.

| head | large | poor | though | wash |

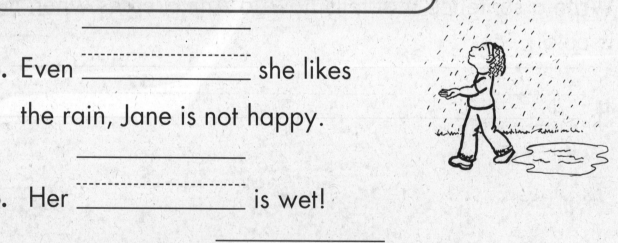

5. Even _____ she likes

the rain, Jane is not happy.

6. Her _____ is wet!

7. She stepped in a _____ puddle too!

 School + Home

Home Activity This page helps your child learn to read and write the words *head, large, poor, though,* and *wash.* Work through the items with your child. For practice, have your child create a story using the words.

© Pearson Education B

Name _____

| sunny | rainy | windy | snowy |

A. Look at the pictures about weather. **Choose** two. **Write** the name of each in the chart. Under the name, **write** details about that kind of weather.

_____   _____

- - - - - - - - - - - - - - - - -   - - - - - - - - - - - - - - - - -

_____   _____

1. _____   **3.** _____

- - - - - - - - - - - - - - - -   - - - - - - - - - - - - - - - -

_____   _____

- - - - - - - - - - - - - - - -   - - - - - - - - - - - - - - - -

2. _____   **4.** _____

B. Write sentences telling how the two types of weather are the same and not the same. Use details from your chart.

_____

- -

_____

- -

_____

Home Activity This page helps your child write sentences comparing two kinds of weather. Discuss a time when a change in weather changed plans you had.

Name_____

Say the word for each picture. **Use** two words to make a compound word that stands for the picture.

Write the compound word on the line.

tea + pot = teapot

---

1. lunch + box

_____

_____

2. back + pack

_____

_____

---

3. rain + bow

_____

_____

4. base + ball

_____

_____

Find the word that you can put together with *light* to make a compound word. **Mark** the ⬭ to show your answer. **Write** the word on the line.

_____

----

5. _____light
 ⬭ kick
 ⬭ pass
 ⬭ moon

_____

----

6. light_____
 ⬭ rain
 ⬭ meal
 ⬭ bulb

© Pearson Education B

Home Activity The activity uses compound words that are made of two smaller words, such as *bankbook*. Point to things in your home with names that are compound words, such as *doorknob*, *raincoat*, and *dishwasher*. Help your child name each object and write its name.

98 **Phonics** Compound Words

Practice Book Unit 5

Name_____

Read the story. **Answer** the questions.

It takes lots of workers to build a house. One person makes the plans. A foreman reads the plans. He tells his workers how to follow the plans. "Put this wall here," he'll say. "Put that window there." Step by step, they do a good job. It takes lots of workers to build a house.

1. Which group of words tells the main idea?
   lots of workers   put this wall here

2. Which word gives a detail about the main idea?
   window   foreman

3. Write the sentence that tells the main idea.

_____

- -

_____

4. In the story, who is one worker that helps build a house?
   ⬭ a foreman
   ⬭ a teacher
   ⬭ a banker

Home Activity The page practices identifying the main idea and supporting details in a story. Describe the process of building something, like a sand castle or fort. Have your child identify the main idea and details.

Circle the word that matches each clue.

1. what you read hold book	**2.** a part of something piece listen
3. to hear listen book	**4.** to have in your hand hold heard

Pick a word from the box to finish each sentence.
Write the word on the line.

┌───┐
│ **listen   hold   book   piece   heard** │
└───┘

5. It is time to read from the big _____ .

6. Mr. Lopez will _____ it up so we can see!

7. We will _____ to Mr. Lopez read.

8. I have never _____ this story before.

9. It's about a cat who takes a _____ of cake.

10. We have this _____ in a small size too.

Home Activity This page helps your child learn to read and write the words *book, heard, hold, listen,* and *piece.* Work through the items with your child. Then dictate each word to your child. Have him or her say each letter aloud while writing.

© Pearson Education B

Name_____

List jobs that you do at home. Under each job, **write** two sentences that tell why it is good to do each job well.

1. Job _____

_____

_____

_____

2. Job _____

_____

_____

_____

3. Job _____

_____

_____

_____

© Pearson Education B

Home Activity This page helps your child write sentences. Discuss the ways your child helps at home and the reasons why it is important to do a good job. Talk with your child about the jobs done by other members of the family.

Name_____

Read the word that is formed
from each pair of syllables.
Write the word on the line.

ap + ple   ta + ble
apple   table

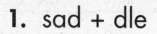

1. sad + dle

_____

_____

2. ca + ble

_____

----

3. Un + cle

_____

_____

4. lit + tle

_____

Pick a word from above to finish each sentence.
Write the word on the line.

_____

----

5. My _____ Jim has a
horse named Jack.

_____

----

6. I give Jack an _____ .

 Home Activity This page practices words with open syllables (those that end in a vowel) and closed
syllables (those that end in a consonant). These words all end in *le*. Write *kettle*, *bottle*, *table*, and *bugle* on
index cards. Have your child draw a line between the two syllables in each word.

Name _____

Read the story. **Look** at the pictures.
Write 1, 2, 3, 4 to show the right order.

I have a dog named Buddy. First thing in the morning, I put on his leash. Then we go for a brisk run. When we get home, I give Buddy some water. I take my shower, and then we eat a little something. He gets dog food and I get oatmeal with apple.

I give Buddy water.

We eat something.

We run.

I put on Buddy's leash.

----

5. Write a sentence that tells what might happen next.

_____

_____

School + Home

Home Activity The activity works with the sequence of events in a story. Work with your child to write about taking care of a pet. Have your child make a drawing to go with the story.

Name_____

Pick a word from the box to finish each sentence.
Write it on the line.

| several   either   boy   you're   hundred |

_____
1. A _____ and his dad were
selling pups, so we got one.

_____
2. We can feed him _____
dry dog food or wet dog food.

_____
3. I have to walk him _____ times a day.

_____
4. There are a _____ other things I have to do!

_____
5. I think _____ wondering how I can do it all!

Pick a word to match each clue. **Mark** the ⬯ to show
your answer.

6. several
  ⬯ divided
  ⬯ none
  ⬯ many

7. you're
  ⬯ you are
  ⬯ your
  ⬯ you aren't

8. hundred
  ⬯ 99 + 3
  ⬯ 99 + 1
  ⬯ 99 + 5

© Pearson Education B

Home Activity This page helps your child learn to read and write the words *boy*, *either*, *hundred*, *several*, and *you're*. Work through the items with your child. For practice, have your child use each word in a sentence.

Name _____

A. Imagine that you will take a pet home to live with you. **Tell** what animal you will pick.

_____

My Pet _____

B. What will your pet need? **Write** five sentences to tell how you will take care of it.

_____

1. _____

_____

2. _____

_____

3. _____

_____

4. _____

_____

5. _____

Home Activity This page helps your child write sentences. Think about different things animals need. Help your child write sentences and draw pictures about taking care of animals.

Name_____

Say the word for each picture.
Write ou or **ow** to finish the word.

m**ou**se   c**ow**

1. cl____n

2. c____ch

3. cr____n

4. cl____d

5. fl____er

6. h____se

7.  gr____nd

8.  ____l

Find the word that rhymes with the picture.
Mark the ⬭ to show your answer.

9. ⬭ south
⬭ loud
⬭ how

10. ⬭ town
⬭ cow
⬭ proud

Home Activity This page practices words with the *ou* and *ow* sound in *mouse* and *cow*. Work through the items with your child. Then together think of two or more words that contain this sound.

Name_____

quick + ly = quick**ly**
play + ful = play**ful**

| beautiful | helpful | slowly |
| neatly | grateful | |

Pick a word from the box to finish each sentence.
Write the word on the line.

1. I like to help around the house.

   _____

   I want to be _____ .

2. The first day I made my bed, I did not go fast.

   _____

   I went _____ .

3. It was a bit messy.

   _____

   Now I make my bed _____ .

4. Mom is _____ for my help.

5. My room looks _____ !

Home Activity The page works with words with the suffixes *-ly* and *-ful*. With your child, make a simple list of rules for your family that contain words with the suffixes *-ly* and *-ful*, such as be helpful, shut doors quietly, walk slowly.

© Pearson Education B

Name_____

Read the story.
Write your answers on the lines.

In the fall, we get lots of apples from our
tree. Mom needs a big ladder. She tosses the apples to
my sister and me. We put them in big bags. When the
bags are full, it's time to get to work. My sister and I
wash the apples. Mom peels and chops them. They go
in a big pot. Mom adds spices to the mix. She puts the
pot on the stove. This will taste so good! All we have to
do is wait!

1. Why does Mom need a big ladder?

_____

- -

_____

2. Why does Mom put the pot on the stove?

_____

- -

_____

3. What will the girls do with the apples in the pot?

_____

- -

_____

© Pearson Education B

Home Activity The page asks your child to draw conclusions. Work with your child to write about a job
that you do together. Think of how to enjoy a job well done.

Name_____

Pick a word from the box to finish each sentence.
Write the word on the line.

| ago   break   certain   probably   since |

1. A week _____ , Dad got
   this nice vase.

2. He will _____ fill it with flowers from
   our yard.

3. Our job is to make _____ the vase is safe.

4. He does not want it to _____ .

5. We don't play ball in the house _____ Dad
   got the vase.

© Pearson Education B

Home Activity This page helps your child learn to read and write the words *ago, break, certain, probably,* and *since.* Work through the items with your child. For practice, have your child use each word in a sentence.

Name_____

A. Think about something you did that helped your family. In the chart, write details about what you did.

How I Helped My Family _____

_____

_____

_____

_____

_____

_____

B. Write sentences to tell what you did.

_____

_____

_____

_____

_____

© Pearson Education B

Home Activity This page helps your child write sentences. Think about ways that your child helps your family. Help your child write a sentence about it.

Name_____

Circle the word for each picture.
Write the word on the line.

b<u>oo</u>t    sp<u>oo</u>n

1. moon   man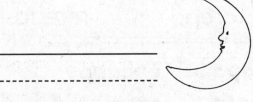
   _____
   - - - - - - - - - - - - -
   _____

2. cool   broom
   _____
   - - - - - - - - - - - - -
   _____

3. tool   tooth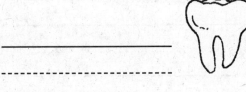
   _____
   - - - - - - - - - - - - -
   _____

4. pool   pole
   _____
   - - - - - - - - - - - - -
   _____

Find the word that rhymes with the picture name.
Mark the ⬯ to show your answer.

5. ⬯ too
   ⬯ spoon
   ⬯ spin

6. ⬯ boom
   ⬯ box
   ⬯ hoot

School + Home **Home Activity** The activity uses words that have the sound of *oo* as in *moon*. Encourage your child to think of words that rhyme with *moon* and *pool*. Together, use the words to create a rhyme.

Name_____

Pick a word from the box to match the meaning.
Write it on the line.

clean   unclean

read   reread

| reread | unsafe | repaint | unhappy |
| retell | unpack | untie | retie |

1. read again

_____

2. not safe

_____

3. tie again

_____

4. undo a tie

_____

5. tell again

_____

6. paint one more time

_____

7. opposite of pack

_____

8. not happy

_____

© Pearson Education B

School + Home   **Home Activity** The activity uses words that begin with *un-* or *re-*, such as *untie* and *repaint*. With your child, say and act out the meaning of these words: *tie, untie, retie; pack, unpack, repack; read, reread; happy, unhappy; safe, unsafe.*

Name_____

Read the sentences. **Write** your answers on the lines.

1. Mr. Sims shakes hands with Glen. They are friends now. Will Mr. Sims talk to Glen another day?

_____
- -
_____

2. Glen greets Mr. Sims each day. How does Glen feel about Mr. Sims?

_____
- -
_____

3. Mr. Sims has a plum tree. He gives a big bag of plums to Glen's family. Why does he do this?

_____
- -
_____

4. Glen's mom makes plum jam. Glen's mom ties a ribbon around a jar of jam. Then she takes it outside. Where is she going?

_____
- -
_____

School + Home **Home Activity** This page helps your child use text to draw conclusions. Read an article together from a children's magazine. Encourage your child to talk about what is happening. Ask him or her to draw conclusions.

Name_____

Circle the word that matches each clue.
Write the word on the line.

1. Today we visited Mr. Lin. We have

_____

_____ there before.   been   course

2. I went with my big

_____

_____ .   course   brother

3. Mom made a

_____

_____ pie for him.   special   been

4. Mr. Lin is the nicest man on the

_____

_____ block.   whole   been

_____

----

5. Of _____ we

like him!   course   brother

© Pearson Education B

Home Activity This page helps your child learn to read and write the words *been, brother, course, special,* and *whole.* Work through the items with your child. For practice, have your child expand the story using the same words.

Name_____

Write about the things good neighbors do for each other.
Use words in the box if you want.

| helpful | friendly | work | nice | special | enjoy |

1. Good neighbors _____ .

2. _____

3. _____

4. _____

5. _____

© Pearson Education B

Home Activity This page helps your child finish sentences and learn to write sentences. Ask your child to tell about being a good neighbor.

Name_____

Read each sentence.
Circle the word with the **/oi/** sound as in **oil** and **toy**.
Write the word on the line.

We <u>oi</u>led my <u>toy</u> car.

_____

1. My car was making a lot of noise. _____

2. It was starting to annoy me. _____

3. Dad helps me take care of my toys. _____

4. We clean off the soil. _____

5. Then we put oil on the wheels. _____

6. Now I enjoy riding it! _____

© Pearson Education B

Home Activity This page uses words that have the diphthongs *oi* and *oy*. Ask your child to read the story of the toy car to you and then draw a picture to go with the story. Work together to label the picture.

Name_____

Pick a word from the box to finish each sentence.
Write the word on the line.

| know   write   wrong   lamb   knit |

1. I need to _____ a story for school.

2. I _____ what I want to write.

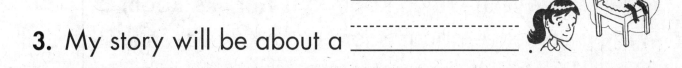

3. My story will be about a _____ .

4. My lamb will _____ a scarf.

5. If I write something _____ ,
   I will fix it.

Home Activity This page uses words that contain silent consonants as in *kn*, *wr*, and *mb*. Discuss and help your child write other words that contain these consonants, such as *thumb*, *knot*, *knock*, *wrap*, and *wrist*. Help your child use each word in a sentence.

chairs   neat   mess   toys   rules   put   away

Look for ways in which Room 5 is **not** like Room 6.
Write a sentence about Room 5. The words in the box
may help you.

_____

1. _____

Look for ways in which Room 6 is **not** like Room 5.
Write a sentence about Room 6. The words in the box
may help you.

_____

2. _____

Write a sentence that tells how Rooms 5 and 6 are
the same.

_____

3. _____

 Home Activity The activity asks your child to describe how two classrooms are the same and different. Ask
your child to compare and contrast two rooms in your house.

© Pearson Education B

Name_____

Pick a word from the box
to finish each sentence.
Write it on the line.

| hour   leave   minute   sorry   watch |

1. I need to _____ for a school meeting.

2. The meeting starts in one _____ .
   That's 60 seconds!

3. I am so _____ that I will be late.

4. Li, please _____ Carla while I'm away.

5. I will be back in about an _____ .

Pick a word from the box to match the clue.
Write the word on the line.

6. to go _____

Home Activity This page helps your child learn to read and write the words *hour, leave, minute, sorry,* and *watch.* Work through the items with your child. For practice, take turns with your child saying other sentences that use these words.

Practice Book Unit 5   **High-Frequency Words** **119**

Name_____

Think of a time when you had to decide what was the right thing to do. **Describe** what you had to decide.

_____

1. _____

_____

_____

Write 4 sentences that tell what you did and why.

_____

2. _____

_____

3. _____

_____

4. _____

_____

5. _____

School + Home

Home Activity This page helps your child write sentences about making a decision. Ask your child to tell about the decision he or she wrote about. Ask why your child thought it was the right thing to do.

Name_____

Read each sentence. **Circle** the word with the same vowel sound as b<u>oo</u>k.
Write the word on the line.   b<u>oo</u>k

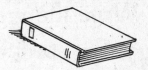

1. Joan went for a walk in the woods.   _____

2. She found a noisy brook.   _____

3. She stood by the rushing water.   _____

4. Joan looked at the frog and fish.   _____

5. A cool breeze shook the leaves on the trees.   _____

6. Joan took home a leaf to remember her walk.   _____

Home Activity This activity practices words with the vowel sound of *oo* in *book*. Work through the items with your child. Write the word ending *ook* on paper. Have your child add beginning letters to form words.

© Pearson Education B

Name_____

Pick a word from the box to match each picture.
Write the word on the line.

paint + er = paint**er**   visit + or = visit**or**

actor	builder	camper	catcher
farmer	sailor	teacher	waiter

1.

_____

- - - - - - - - - - - - - - - - - - -

_____

2.

_____

- - - - - - - - - - - - - - - - - - -

_____

3.

_____

- - - - - - - - - - - - - - - - - - -

_____

4.

_____

- - - - - - - - - - - - - - - - - - -

_____

5.

_____

- - - - - - - - - - - - - - - - - - -

_____

6.

_____

- - - - - - - - - - - - - - - - - - -

_____

© Pearson Education B

School + Home

Home Activity This activity practices words with the suffixes -er and -or. Work through the items with your child. Help your child write sentences using the words from this page.

Name_____

Tennis   **Volleyball**

Look for ways in which tennis is **not** like volleyball.
Write two sentences about tennis.

1. _____

2. _____

Write one sentence that tells how both sports are alike.

3. _____

Look for ways in which volleyball is **not** like tennis.
Write two sentences about volleyball.

4. _____

5. _____

Home Activity Have your child describe ways in which two sports are alike and different. Work through the items with your child. Together, talk about how two other sports are alike and different.

Practice Book Unit 6   **Comprehension** Compare and Contrast **123**

Name_____

Pick a word from the box to finish each sentence.
Write the word on the line.

| bought | buy | clothes | won | worst |

1. Sofia needed to _____ new sports things.

2. Last week she _____ ice skates.

3. She also got _____ for skating.

4. Sofia _____ a prize for her skating.

Pick a word that is the opposite of each word below.
Mark the space to show your answer.

5. best
   - ⬭ even
   - ⬭ worst
   - ⬭ good

6. lost
   - ⬭ stay
   - ⬭ few
   - ⬭ won

Home Activity This page helps your child read and write the words *bought, buy, clothes, won,* and *worst.*
Work through the items with your child. Ask your child to tell about something he or she has bought, using
some of the words in the box.

Name_____

Complete the chart. **Write** three details about each sport.

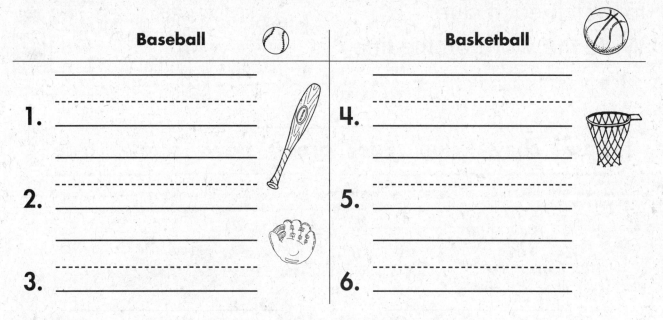

Baseball	Basketball
1. _____	4. _____
2. _____	5. _____
3. _____	6. _____

Write two sentences to tell how the sports are alike.
Write two sentences to tell how the sports are different.
Use some of your ideas from the chart.

7. _____

8. _____

9. _____

10. _____

Home Activity This page helps your child practice writing sentences that tell how two sports are alike and different. Help your child write the sentences. On a separate sheet of paper, help your child write two more sentences that tell how the sports are alike and two more sentences that tell how they are different.

Practice Book Unit 6

Writing 125

Name_____

Pick a word from the box
to match each clue.
Write the word on the line.

bl<u>ew</u>  gl<u>ue</u>

| blue   chew   clue   Sue   grew   new   screw   true |

1.

_____

- - - - - - - - - - - - - - - -

2.

_____

- - - - - - - - - - - - - - - -

3. use your teeth

_____

- - - - - - - - - - - - - - - -

4. not false

_____

- - - - - - - - - - - - - - - -

5. got larger in size

_____

- - - - - - - - - - - - - - - -

6. a color

_____

- - - - - - - - - - - - - - - -

7. a girl's name

_____

- - - - - - - - - - - - - - - -

8. not old

_____

- - - - - - - - - - - - - - - -

 Home Activity This activity practices words with the vowel patterns *ew* as in *blew* and *ue* as in *glue*. Work through the items with your child. Then help your child write these words and tell what they mean: *news, drew, stew, true, clue.*

Name_____

Add pre- or dis- to each word to make a new word.
Write the new word on the line.

pre + heat = **pre**heat

dis + connect = **dis**connect

Add pre

1. wash

_____

_____

2. game

_____

_____

Add dis

3. please

_____

_____

4. trust

_____

_____

Write a sentence using each word.

5. preplan _____
_____

6. dislike _____

© Pearson Education B

Home Activity This page practices words with the prefixes *pre-* and *dis-*. Work through the items with your child. Have your child read each word on the page and tell its meaning.

Practice Book Unit 6

Phonics Prefixes *pre-*, *dis-* **127**

Name_____

Look at the pictures. **Read** the steps.
Write a number from **1** to **5** to show
the right order.

_____

_____ Next, hook the flag on to the clips.

_____

_____ Second, stretch out the flag.

_____

_____ At last, the flag is at the top.

_____

_____ Then, pull the rope on the flagpole.

_____

_____ First, get the flag from the shelf.

© Pearson Education B

School + Home **Home Activity** Your child puts the steps of a process in the right order. Work through the items with your child. Ask your child to say the steps in order.

128 **Comprehension** Sequence

Practice Book Unit 6

Name_____

Pick a word from the box to match each clue.
Write the word on the line.

air   America   beautiful   Earth   world

1.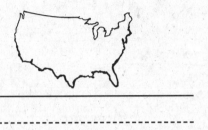

_____

- - - - - - - - - - - - - - - -

_____

2.

_____

- - - - - - - - - - - - - - - -

_____

- - - - - - - - - - - - - - - -

3. We live on the planet called _____ .

4. Another word for pretty is _____ .

Write the word from the box that fits the clue.

_____

- - - - - - - - - - - - - - - -

5. another word for the planet Earth _____

_____

- - - - - - - - - - - - - - - -

6. the name of our planet _____

Home Activity This page helps your child read and write the words *air, America, beautiful, earth,* and *world*. Work through the items with your child. For practice, have your child look at each word in the box, read it, and spell it. Take turns using the words in sentences.

© Pearson Education B

Name_____

Write an answer to each question.

Question	Answer
1. How do you feel when you see the American flag? →	
2. How do you show that you care about the flag? →	

Write two sentences that tell what the American flag means to you.

3. _____

_____

4. _____

Did I begin each sentence with a capital letter? ⬭ yes ⬭ no

Did I use the correct mark at the end of each sentence? ⬭ yes ⬭ no

Did I use good words to describe my feelings? ⬭ yes ⬭ no

© Pearson Education B

Home Activity This page helps your child write sentences about the American flag. Help your child write the sentences. Then read the sentences together.

Name_____

Write the contraction on the line.

⑤

You are five.
You're five.

---

1. we have

_____

- - - - - - - - - - - - - -

_____

2. she would

_____

- - - - - - - - - - - - - -

_____

---

3. they are

_____

- - - - - - - - - - - - - -

_____

4. I would

_____

- - - - - - - - - - - - - -

_____

---

5. they have

_____

- - - - - - - - - - - - - -

_____

6. we are

_____

- - - - - - - - - - - - - -

_____

Find the contraction for each pair of words.
Mark the space to show your answer.

7. I have
- ⬭ I've
- ⬭ I'd
- ⬭ I'll

8. we would
- ⬭ we're
- ⬭ we'd
- ⬭ we've

School + Home

Home Activity This activity practices words with contractions *'re, 've, 'd*. Help your child make a set of flashcards with a word pair (such as *you are*) on one side and the matching contraction (such as *you're*) on the other. Use the flashcards to practice the contractions.

Name _____

Say the word for each picture. **Write ph** or **dge** to finish each word.

ele**ph**ant   ba**dge**

---

1.    **2.**    **3.**    **4.**

bri_____   ple_____   gra_____   ju_____

---

5.   **6.**    **7.**    **8.**

go_____er   he_____   dol_____in   _____oto

Write a sentence using each word.

_____

9. trophy _____

_____

10. edge _____

© Pearson Education B

 Home Activity This activity practices words with the sound of *ph* as in *elephant* and *dge* as in *fudge*. Work through the items with your child. Point to the words your child wrote on the page. Ask your child to read each word and use the word in a sentence that tells about each picture.

Name_____

Read the story. **Look** at the picture. **Follow** the directions.

Today I turn eight. My father is baking a special cake. My sister is hanging up streamers. My friends will come to our house this afternoon. Then we will eat cake and drink punch. We will play games. I will unwrap my gifts. It will be a fun day.

Circle the word that best finishes each sentence.
Write the word on the line.

wedding   birthday
_____

1. It is the boy's _____ .

contest   party
_____

2. His family is having a _____ .

3. **Write** a sentence to tell how the boy feels.

_____

_____

Home Activity Your child reads a story and draws conclusions from the information in the story. Together, read a story. Pause to ask open-ended questions, such as "What's going on now?" and "What's this all about?"

© Pearson Education B

Name_____

Pick a word from the box to finish each sentence.
Write the word on the line.

| believe | company | everybody | money | young |

1. My family pays _____ for a new swimming pool.

2. We invite _____ we know to come swim.

3. The _____ children splash and play.

4. Our _____ stays all afternoon.

5. I _____ they had fun at our new pool.

Home Activity This page helps your child read and write the words *believe, company, everybody, money,* and *young.* Work through the items with your child. Ask your child to retell the story on this page, using each of the words from the box.

© Pearson Education B

Name_____

Write about a special family celebration. Write notes in the chart. Then use your notes to write sentences about the celebration.

Kind of celebration	
Place and time	
People who were there	
What we did	
What we ate	
Why it was special	

_____

- -

_____

- -

_____

Home Activity This page helps your child write sentences about a special family celebration. Help your child recall details of the celebration and write them in the chart. Then help your child use the details to write sentences. Read the sentences together.

Name_____

Pick a word from the box to match each clue.
Write the word on the line.

br**ea**d

breakfast	breath	feather	head	heavy
instead	ready	spread	thread	

1.

_____

- - - - - - - - - - -

_____

2.

_____

- - - - - - - - - - -

_____

3.

_____

- - - - - - - - - - -

_____

4. morning meal

_____

- - - - - - - - - - -

_____

5. in the place of

_____

- - - - - - - - - - -

_____

6. not light

_____

- - - - - - - - - - -

_____

Unscramble the letters to make a word from the box.
Write the word on the line.

7. darey

_____

- - - - - - - - - - -

8. aspedr

_____

- - - - - - - - - - -

9. traebh

_____

- - - - - - - - - - -

© Pearson Education B

Home Activity This activity practices words with *ea* as in *bread*. Work through the items with your child.
Help your child use each word on this page in a sentence.

Name_____

Add the prefixes and suffixes to the words.
Write the new words on the lines.
Use the words in the box if you need help.

re + cycle = **re**cycle

discontinue	**hungrily**	**luckiest**	**painful**
preorder	**rewritten**	**thinner**	**unhappiest**

1. lucky + est

_____

- - - - - - - - - - - - - - - - - -

_____

2. re + written

_____

- - - - - - - - - - - - - - - - - -

_____

3. thin + er

_____

- - - - - - - - - - - - - - - - - -

4. hungry + ly

_____

- - - - - - - - - - - - - - - - - -

Pick a word from the box to match each clue.
Write the word on the line.

5. full of hurt

_____

- - - - - - - - - - - - - - - - - -

6. most sad

_____

- - - - - - - - - - - - - - - - - -

© Pearson Education B

School + Home **Home Activity** This activity practices base words and affixes. Work through the items with your child. Together, look for words like these in ads and signs. Help your child pronounce the words and figure out what they mean. Encourage your child to use the meanings of the prefixes and suffixes to help define the words.

Name_____

Look for ways in which the cowboy hat is **not** like the baseball cap. **Write** two sentences about the cowboy hat.

1. _____

2. _____

Write one sentence that tells how these two hats are alike.

3. _____

Look for ways in which the baseball cap is **not** like the cowboy hat. **Write** two sentences about the baseball cap.

4. _____

5. _____

© Pearson Education B

 Home Activity Have your child describe ways in which a cowboy hat and a baseball cap are the same and different. Work through the items with your child. Together, compare other items of clothing. Ask your child to describe what is the same and different about the items of clothing.

138 **Comprehension** Compare and Contrast   **Practice Book Unit 6**

Name_____

| alone | between | notice | question | woman |

Write a word from the box that means almost the same as each word below.

1. among

_____

- - - - - - - - - - - - - - - - - - - -

_____

2. see

_____

- - - - - - - - - - - - - - - - - - - -

_____

Write a word from the box that is the opposite of each word below.

3. man

_____

- - - - - - - - - - - - - - - - - - - -

_____

4. answer

_____

- - - - - - - - - - - - - - - - - - - -

_____

Write a word from the box to finish each sentence.

5. A _____ went to the barn.

6. She did not _____ the sign out front.

7. She was all _____ in the barn.

Home Activity This page helps your child read and write the words *alone, between, notice, question,* and *woman.* Work through the items with your child. Make a "word file" box for your child out of a shoebox. Provide paper or index cards to write and illustrate new words.

© Pearson Education B

Name_____

Complete the chart. **Write** two details about cowboys long ago and cowboys today.

A Cowboy's Life Long Ago	A Cowboy's Life Today
1. _____	3. _____
2. _____	4. _____

Write a sentence to tell how a cowboy's life today is like a cowboy's life long ago. **Write** a sentence to tell how their lives are different. **Use** some of your ideas from the chart.

5. _____

6. _____

Did I begin each sentence with a capital letter? ⬭ yes ⬭ no

Did I use the correct mark at the end of each sentence? ⬭ yes ⬭ no

Did I use good describing words? ⬭ yes ⬭ no

© Pearson Education B

Home Activity This page helps your child practice writing sentences that tell about a cowboy's life long ago and today. On a separate sheet of paper, help your child write two more sentences that tell how a cowboy's life long ago was like or different from a cowboy's life today.

Name_____

Say the word for each picture. **Write** the word on the
line. **Use** the words in the box if you need help.

dr**aw**   f**au**cet   t**augh**t

| auto   caught   daughter   launch   straw   yawn |

1.

_____
- - - - - - - - - - - - - -
_____

2.

_____
- - - - - - - - - - - - - -
_____

3.

_____
- - - - - - - - - - - - - -
_____

4.

_____
- - - - - - - - - - - - - -
_____

5.

_____
- - - - - - - - - - - - - -
_____

6.

_____
- - - - - - - - - - - - - -
_____

School + Home **Home Activity** This activity practices words with *aw* as in *draw*, *au* as in *faucet*, and *augh* as in *taught*.
Work through the items with your child. Then say a word from this page. Have your child repeat the word
and tell what letters spell the vowel sound.

Name_____

Read each word.
Find the base word.
Write the base word on the line.

loud**ly**

---

1. happier _____

2. distrustful _____

3. wider _____

4. easily _____

5. unsafely _____

6. thankfully _____

7. silliest _____

8. editor _____

Add the prefixes and suffixes to the words. **Write** the new words on the lines.

9. flat + est
_____

10. un + beaten
_____

11. survive + or
_____

12. joy + ful + ly
_____

© Pearson Education B

Home Activity This activity practices base words and affixes. Work through the items with your child. Read a story with your child. Look for words with prefixes and suffixes.

Name_____

Look at the e-mail. Write the answer to each question.

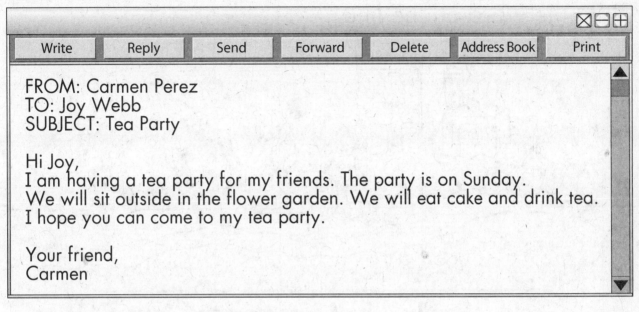

1. Who is this e-mail from?

_____
- -
_____

_ _ _ _ _ _ _ _ _ _

2. What is the subject of the e-mail? _____

_ _ _ _ _ _ _ _ _ _ _

3. Which button do you click to answer? _____

Write two details that tell more about the subject.

_____

4. _____

_____

5. _____

Home Activity Have your child identify the subject and details of an e-mail message. Work through the items with your child. Write a pretend e-mail together. Include the subject and some details that tell more about the subject.

Practice Book Unit 6   **Comprehension** Main Idea and Supporting Details   **143**

Name_____

Pick a word from the box to finish each sentence.
Write the word on the line.

cold	finally	half	tomorrow	word

1. The town newspaper gets the _____ out.

2. It is _____ the week for the winter party.

3. The party will begin _____ .

4. The weather is _____ and snowy.

5. More than _____ the townspeople will be there.

 Home Activity This page helps your child read and write the words *cold, finally, half, tomorrow,* and *word.* Work through the items with your child. Write each word on an index card or paper. Have your child pick a card, read the word, and use it in a sentence.

© Pearson Education B

Name_____

Write an answer to each question.

Question		Answer
1. What celebration do you like?	→	_____
2. What did you do?	→	_____
3. How did you feel?	→	_____

Write a sentence about each question you answered.

4. _____

5. _____

6. _____

Did I begin each sentence with a capital letter? ⬭ yes ⬭ no

Did I use the correct mark at the end of each sentence? ⬭ yes ⬭ no

Did I use good words to describe my feelings? ⬭ yes ⬭ no

Home Activity This page helps your child write sentences about a celebration. Help your child recall other details and write additional sentences. Then read the sentences together.

Name

I read

It was about

Words I Can Now Read and Write

Name_____

I read _____

_____

_____

It was about

Words I Can Now Read and Write

_____ _____

_____ _____

_____ _____

Name_____

I read _____

_____

_____

It was about

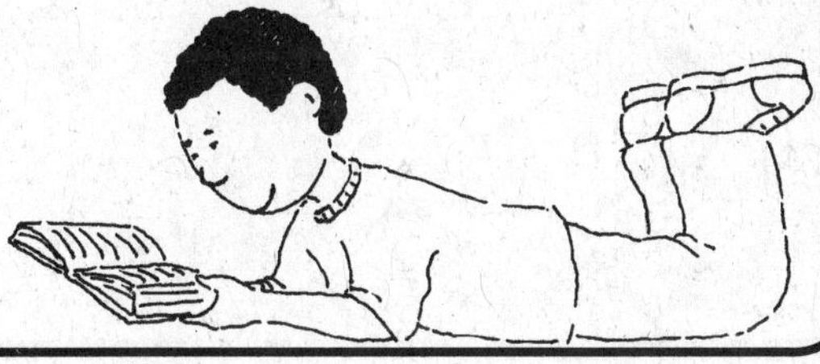

Words I Can Now Read and Write

_____ _____

_____ _____

Name _____

I read _____

_____

It was about

Words I Can Now Read and Write

_____   _____

_____   _____

Name

I read

It was about

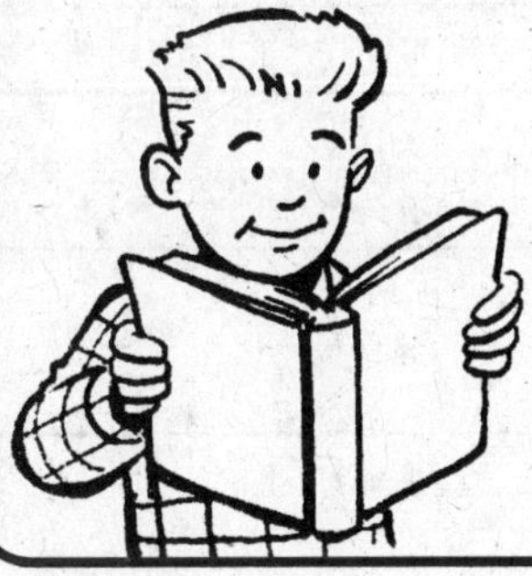

Words I Can Now Read and Write

Name_____

Words I Can Now Read and Write

_____ _____
- - - - - - - - - - - - - - - - - - - - - - - - - -
_____ _____

_____ _____
- - - - - - - - - - - - - - - - - - - - - - - - - -
_____ _____

_____ _____
- - - - - - - - - - - - - - - - - - - - - - - - - -
_____ _____

_____ _____
- - - - - - - - - - - - - - - - - - - - - - - - - -
_____ _____

_____ _____
- - - - - - - - - - - - - - - - - - - - - - - - - -
_____ _____

_____ _____
- - - - - - - - - - - - - - - - - - - - - - - - - -
_____ _____

_____

Name_____

Words I Can Now Read and Write

_____   _____
- - - - - - - - - - - - - -   - - - - - - - - - - - - - -
_____   _____

_____   _____
- - - - - - - - - - - - - -   - - - - - - - - - - - - - -
_____   _____

_____   _____
- - - - - - - - - - - - - -   - - - - - - - - - - - - - -
_____   _____

_____   _____
- - - - - - - - - - - - - -   - - - - - - - - - - - - - -
_____   _____

_____   _____
- - - - - - - - - - - - - -   - - - - - - - - - - - - - -
_____   _____

_____   _____
- - - - - - - - - - - - - -   - - - - - - - - - - - - - -
_____   _____

_____
- - - - - - - - - - - - - -
_____

Name_____

Words I Can Now Read and Write

_____   _____
- - - - - - - - - - - - - - - - -   - - - - - - - - - - - - - - - - -
_____   _____
- - - - - - - - - - - - - - - - -   - - - - - - - - - - - - - - - - -
_____   _____

_____   _____
- - - - - - - - - - - - - - - - -   - - - - - - - - - - - - - - - - -
_____   _____
- - - - - - - - - - - - - - - - -   - - - - - - - - - - - - - - - - -
_____   _____

_____   _____
- - - - - - - - - - - - - - - - -   - - - - - - - - - - - - - - - - -
_____   _____
- - - - - - - - - - - - - - - - -   - - - - - - - - - - - - - - - - -
_____   _____

_____   _____
- - - - - - - - - - - - - - - - -

Practice Book

Name_____

Words I Can Now Read and Write